The Illusion of Difference

Realities of Ethnicity in Canada and the United States

Jeffrey G. Reitz
and
Raymond Breton

D1248687

Observation 37
C.D. Howe Institute

C.D. Howe Institute publications are available from:
Renouf Publishing Company Limited, 1294 Algoma Road,
Ottawa, Ontario K1B 3W8; phone (613) 741-4333; fax (613) 741-5439

and from Renouf's stores at:
71½ Sparks Street, Ottawa (613) 238-8985
211 Yonge Street, Toronto (416) 363-3171

For trade book orders, please contact:
McGraw-Hill Ryerson Limited, 300 Water Street,
Whitby, Ontario L1N 9B6; phone (416) 430-5050

Institute publications are also available in microform from:
Micromedia Limited, 165 Hôtel de Ville, Place du Portage, Phase II,
Hull, Quebec J8X 3X2

This book is printed on recycled, acid-free paper.

Canadian Cataloguing in Publication Data

Reitz, Jeffrey G.
    The illusion of difference : realities of
ethnicity in Canada and the United States

(Observation, ISSN 0826-9947 ; no. 37)
Includes bibliographical references.
ISBN 0-88806-342-3

1. Ethnicity – Canada. 2. Ethnicity – United States.
3. Canada – Ethnic relations. 4. United States –
Ethnic relations. 5. Multiculturalism – Canada.
6. Assimilation (Sociology). I. Breton, Raymond,
1931– . II. C.D. Howe Institute. III. Title. IV. Series:
Observation (C.D. Howe Institute) ; no. 37.

FC104.R45 1994   305.8'00971   C94-931368-8
F1035.A1R45 1994

Cover design by Leroux Design Inc.
Printed in Canada by Hignell Printing Limited,
Winnipeg, Manitoba, May 1994.

Contents

Foreword

In distinguishing themselves from Americans, Canadians have long used the language of metaphor to describe their society as a "mosaic" and the United States as a "melting pot." Canadians think of themselves as being more tolerant of racial minorities, more welcoming of newcomers, more respectful of cultural differences than are their neighbors to the south.

But just how different are the two societies in their treatment of minority ethnic groups? In how quickly they assimilate minorities? And what does the experience of minorities in the two countries tell us about the attitudes of Canadians and Americans to racial and cultural differences? As Canadians struggle to come to terms with growing social and economic strains, and to understand the long-term effects of policy choices such as "multiculturalism," it is increasingly important to find answers to these questions.

To undertake the difficult challenge of comparing the cultural myths and realities of Canada and the United States, the C.D. Howe Institute drew on the expertise of two of Canada's most esteemed sociologists, Jeffrey G. Reitz and Raymond Breton, both of whom are Professors of Sociology at the University of Toronto. Their study, the result of an exhaustive review of the available public opinion data, helps bring a picture of Canadians and Americans into clearer focus.

Reitz and Breton find that, contrary to the comfortable assumptions of many Canadians, Americans are, in fact, more likely to favor cultural retention — at least in intent. When examining actual cultural retention, however, as indicated both by subjective measures of ethnic identification and by behavioral measures such as ethnic intermarriages, Reitz and Breton find no systematic differences: assimilation rates and economic opportunities for minorities in the two countries are similar. In fact, the authors contend, there may be only an illusion of difference between Canada and the United States. As they put it in their conclusion,

> The general cultural differences between Canada and the United States imply differences of tone in ethnic and race relations in the two countries. The Canadian style is more low-key than the American; moreover, Canadians have a conscious tradition of "tolerance" that Americans do not have. In terms of their effects on the experiences of minority groups, however, these differences are more apparent than real.

The C.D. Howe Institute's aim in presenting studies such as this is to raise the level of public debate on issues of national interest by presenting diverse points of view — whether or not it agrees with them — in publications that are well researched and well grounded. The Institute hopes that, in so doing, it will give Canadians much to think about, including the information they require to exercise their responsibilities as citizens.

This volume was copy edited by Alexander Scala, and desktop published by Brenda Palmer. The analysis and opinions presented in the study are the responsibility of the authors and do not necessarily reflect the views of the Institute's members or Board of Directors.

Thomas E. Kierans
President and
Chief Executive Officer

Acknowledgments

We received help and advice for this study from a number of sources, which we acknowledge here with gratitude. Ian McKinnon and Michael Sullivan, with the kind permission of Kevin Doyle, then-editor of *Maclean's*, provided the survey data collected by Decima Research Ltd. Peter McIntosh helped to provide the Gallup poll data. Richard Alba, John Berry, Joseph Fletcher, John Kralt, Réjean Lachapelle, Stanley Lieberson, Rick Ponting, Madeline Richard, and Paul Sniderman all provided information or advice on key points. We are grateful for valuable comments and suggestions by James Geschwender, Gillian Stevens, Morton Weinfeld, and researchers of the C.D. Howe Institute, who reviewed a draft manuscript. We also wish to acknowledge the assistance of Valerie Zawilski in accessing library and data archive resources and Richard Bernard in the computer analysis of census data.

Jeffrey G. Reitz
Raymond Breton

Chapter 1

Canadian Beliefs about the Mosaic and the Melting Pot:
A Critique and Research Agenda

Is multiculturalism in Canada a reality, or is it largely a myth? The idea that Canada is a "cultural mosaic" and, as such, fundamentally different from the American "melting pot," is one of the beliefs about Canada most widely held among Canadians. It is based in part on the fact that the Canadian population is diverse in its ethnic and racial composition, and in part on the fact that Canada has multicultural policies at all levels of government. But the idea of Canada as a cultural mosaic goes far deeper than these basic items of demography and government policy. It refers also to the underlying pattern of social relations among the various ethnic and cultural groups in Canadian society. Canadians believe that their everyday treatment of cultural minorities is different from Americans' treatment of cultural minorities. They also believe that the way in which cultural minorities fit into society is not the same in Canada as it is in the United States. But are these beliefs about the distinctive nature of relations among ethnic groups in Canada founded in fact?

This study asks whether there is a basis in fact for the distinction, cherished by Canadians, between the Canadian mosaic and the American melting pot. The question is important because perceptions of national distinctiveness are part of national ideologies. They have significance in political debate. For example, the debate in Canada over issues arising from the globalization of economic relations, such as "continentalism" in the 1970s and, more recently, the Canada-US Free Trade Agreement and the North American Free

Trade Agreement, involves concerns that closer economic ties with the United States will lead to a loss of Canadian identity and distinctiveness. Groups within Canada may have a stake in one description of Canadian society as opposed to another. This partisanship in turn sparks interest in the question of the reality of national distinctiveness. As a matter of fact, this study was initiated in part to explore further the findings of a 1989 poll conducted by Decima Research Ltd. for a special issue of *Maclean's* magazine devoted to the debate over free trade with the United States. Our analysis, presented in Chapter 2, shows among other things that support for immigrant cultural retention is indeed related to support for Canadian independence from the United States. This finding suggests that descriptions of Canadian distinctiveness should not be taken at face value. Rather, they should be evaluated in relation to relevant facts. Our study will show that Canadians have based their acceptance of these beliefs on considerations that do not always correspond to the actual patters of interethnic relations in the two countries.[1]

Note that it is not our purpose to evaluate multicultural policies in Canada, to take a position pro or con. We emphasize this point because of the continuing debate about the merits of these policies, including debate among social scientists.[2] An evaluation might be useful, but it would require a complex methodology that is far beyond the scope of this study. Our purpose is to describe broad features of Canadian and American society. Nevertheless, we hope that, by examining relations among ethnic groups in Canada and the United States, we shall contribute to the public debate on multiculturalism policies.

Our study is concerned primarily with minority groups composed of immigrants and their descendants, since these groups are the primary focus of beliefs about the mosaic and the melting pot. It might be argued that any comparison of interethnic relations in

---

1 Others have made this point. See, for example, Allan Smith 1970; Palmer 1976; and Weinfeld 1981.

2 See, for example, Brotz 1981; Peter 1981; Bibby 1990; and Fleras and Elliott 1992.

Canada and the United States is incomplete if it is restricted in this way. Certainly the United States and Canada have very different histories of interethnic and interracial contact, and any evaluation of the incorporation of minority groups in each country must take these different histories into account. In the United States, the primary issue has been the incorporation of blacks descended from a large slave population abducted in Africa over a period of centuries. The primary issue in Canada, from its conquest by the British to today, has been accommodation between French-speaking and English-speaking groups. The central relation has always been the relation between French Quebec and the rest of Canada, but English-French relations in regions outside Quebec have also been important at one time or another (Breton, 1988, 557–585).

These processes of incorporation and accommodation have continued over many generations, and since the Second World War they have been a major social and political preoccupation in both countries. They are far from complete today. Americans still agonize over the racial polarization of US society, just as Canadians continue to wrestle with French-English relations.[3] Yet to compare black-white relations in the United States with French-English relations in Canada would be like comparing apples and oranges. A systematic comparative assessment would reveal fundamental differences between the two situations. The black-white issue in the United States is primarily economic. The question is how to overcome still-massive disparities in wealth and income. Blacks in the United States have made major strides toward incorporation, in the face of extraordinary obstacles. Yet black-white economic disparity, and the attendant social problems, continue to be depressing in their scale and scope. The French-English issue in Canada is primarily cultural and political, although it has an underlying economic aspect as well. The problem for Canada is to design a federal system that will provide sufficient autonomy for Quebec to ensure that the French language

---

3 For a recent discussion of racial issues in the United States, see Jaynes and Williams 1989. Breton (1988; 1992) discusses the current state of French-English relations in Canada.

and French culture will thrive within a country (and continent) dominated by English. Measures intended to promote French-English accommodation have affected the entire society from coast to coast, and not only is Quebec a prosperous region of Canada but the French language and French culture are very much alive. Yet the possibility persists that the country will split apart. To put the matter in more fundamental terms, the issue in the United States is integration — the full participation on an equal basis of blacks in an institutional system dominated by whites — whereas the issue in Canada is the accommodation of two institutional systems, one dominated by English-speakers, the other by French-speakers (Breton 1978). Given these differences, it is by no means clear how to specify criteria for progress toward incorporation that would apply to both groups.

This difficulty does not extend to minorities composed of immigrants and their descendants. These groups' historical and demographic position in American society is similar to their position in Canadian society. In both the United States and Canada, the incorporation of immigrant minorities has been a significant social issue, and there are many parallels between the positions of the "new immigrant" racial minorities in the two countries. Thus, the incorporation of immigrant minorities offers a meaningful basis for comparing the two societies.[4]

Although our analysis will focus on minorities composed of immigrants and their descendants, it cannot, for several reasons, wholly ignore other groups. For one thing, the incorporation of immigrant minorities takes place in the context of relations among other groups. For another, data for other groups sometimes throw light on the processes or the degree of incorporation of immigrant minorities. This is particularly true, as we shall show, in the case of interracial inequalities. Finally, studies that provide data on matters

---

4 The position of native or aboriginal groups also offers parallels, but the processes of incorporation, in both countries, are much more complex in this case and available data are less amenable to comparative analysis. However, a comprehensive comparison of the incorporation of native peoples in the two countries would make an important contribution to the objectives of this study.

of culture and opportunity do not always make the distinctions that our focus on immigrant minorities requires.

To place our comparative study in its proper context, we shall begin with a brief description of what we consider to be the essential Canadian beliefs about relations among cultural groups in Canada, beliefs that are implicit in the idea of the cultural mosaic.

Canadian Beliefs about Interethnic Relations in Canada and the United States

The cultural mosaic has become an important cultural and political symbol for Canadians. If the frequency with which Canadian politicians, intellectuals, journalists, and commentators invoke this symbol is any guide, it is deeply ingrained in the Canadian psyche. Like all symbols, however, it means different things to different people, and some of these meanings are vague or even contradictory. Nevertheless, there are certain important beliefs about Canada, and about Canada's distinctiveness in relation to the United States, that inform almost all conceptions of the cultural mosaic, whatever other meanings may be attached to it.

One of these beliefs is that minority groups in Canada are encouraged to maintain their distinctive cultures, whereas minority groups in the United States are under pressure to abandon their traditional cultures and "melt" into the broader society. In short, Canadians show tolerance for diversity and even encourage it. Consequently, minority groups in Canada more freely participate in traditional cultural practices, and maintain ethnic community institutions and activities, than do minority groups in the United States.

The maintenance of ethnic diversity would hardly be a valuable feature of a society if it occurred in the context of inequality, or if it resulted in inequalities. Thus, a second Canadian belief is that tolerance for cultural diversity does not imply isolation from the mainstream society. Rather, immigrant minorities, including those that retain their traditional cultures, are not thought to be disadvantaged in the pursuit of a livelihood, or in access to resources such as housing or community services. In other words, Canadians provide a greater degree of equality of opportunity to ethnic minorities than Americans do, regardless of participation in minority community life. Equality of opportunity, by this reckoning, is a distinctively Canadian virtue, in contrast to an American tendency to discriminate against minorities, particularly those that fail to assimilate completely.

Both of these beliefs refer to patters in interethnic relations to which one can apply the tools of systematic empirical social research. In the next section, we shall explore some of the thinking behind these beliefs. We shall then identify the more specific parameters and indicators that we shall use in subsequent chapters to evaluate the validity of the distinction between a Canadian mosaic and an American melting pot.

An Exploration of Popular Thinking

Canadian beliefs about how Canada's treatment of ethnic minorities differs from their treatment in the United States have not arisen in a vacuum. One can point to several easily observable differences between the two countries that seem to support the distinction between a Canadian mosaic and an American melting pot. However, closer examination reveals that these differences are not necessarily valid indicators of how Canadians actually feel about ethnic minorities, or of how ethnic minorities in Canada actually behave. In other words, there are differences between the two societies that may lead to a *perception* of differences in attitudes toward immigrant minorities, but this perception many not reflect the reality. We shall examine five assertions about differences between the two societies.

1. *Ethnic community life is more visible in Canada than it is in the United States.* This contention, though very likely true, does not necessarily support the conclusion that ethnic minorities in Canada are subject to less pressure to assimilate than ethnic minorities in the United States. Studies in both countries have shown that attachments to ethnic communities are more pronounced among immigrants than

they are among their descendants (Lieberson and Waters 1988; Reitz 1980b). Thus, the perception that ethnic minorities are more visible in Canada may simply reflect the fact that immigrants are proportionately far more numerous in Canada. Immigrants constituted 16 percent of the Canadian population in 1991 but only 8 percent of the US population in 1990.

Immigrants in both countries tend to congregate in large cities. In Canada, however, almost all large cities have substantial proportions of immigrants, while in the United States, immigrants are concentrated only in certain cities. The 1991 Canadian census shows that 38 percent of the population of Toronto (the Census Metropolitan Area) was born outside Canada. The other two Canadian cities with populations over 1 million also have large proportions of immigrants — Vancouver has 30 percent, and Montreal has 17 percent. Most smaller Canadian cities also have many immigrants. In Calgary, for example, immigrants account for 20 percent of the population; in Edmonton and Winnipeg, 18 percent; in Hamilton, 24 percent; and in Ottawa-Hull, 15 percent. Of nine Canadian cities with populations over 500,000, only Quebec City has an immigrant population of less than 15 percent (Badets 1993, 10).

In the United States, there are certain major cities in which immigrants constitute comparable proportions of the population, but the more typical large US city has fewer than the typical Canadian city. The 1990 US census shows that, in New York, immigrants account for 26 percent of the population; in Los Angeles, 33 percent; in San Francisco-Oakland, 21 percent; and in Miami, 45 percent — the largest proportion in any major city in either country. Some other large US cities also have significant immigrant populations (Chicago, 12 percent; Washington, 13 percent; Houston, 13 percent; Boston, 12 percent), but Philadelphia has only 5 percent; Detroit, 6 percent; and Dallas, 8 percent.[5] Many other large US cities, such as Baltimore,

---

5 The US data on percentages of immigrants in specific urban areas are based on Standard Metropolitan Statistical Areas (SMSAs, some reconstructed). See United States, Bureau of the Census 1992.

Atlanta, Pittsburgh, St. Louis, and Minneapolis-St. Paul, have even smaller immigrant populations, and a host of US cities comparable in size to Winnipeg or Calgary has only a very small percentage of immigrants.[6] So immigrants are a far more imposing feature of the "average" city in Canada than is the case in the United States.

Furthermore, in those US cities with the greatest ethnic diversity and the largest experience of recent immigration, many observers of demographic trends have questioned the continued relevance of the metaphor of the melting pot, a development that has paralleled the rise of the multiculturalism ideology in Canada. Nathan Glazer and Daniel P. Moynihan expressed the new view as long ago as 1963 in *Beyond the Melting Pot: The Negroes, Puerto Ricans, Jews, Italians and Irish of New York City* ([1963] 1970; see also Hirschman 1983). American public opinion too reflects the change. A recent national poll asked "Is the United States still a melting pot, or do immigrants today maintain their national identity more strongly?" Only 20 percent felt the United States was still a melting pot, and about two-thirds — 66 percent — said that immigrants now maintain their identity.[7]

Clearly, one cannot determine whether it is true that Canada is a mosaic and the United States is a melting pot on the basis of casual observations about the presence of immigrant communities. It is necessary instead to consider whether minorities in Canada are actually under less social pressures than minorities in the United States to abandon ties to ethnic communities and whether Canadian minorities are less likely actually to abandon such ties. In other words, one must examine the actual behavior of both the majorities

---

6 In a sample drawn from the 1980 US census Public Use Microdata file (5 percent A file), the Baltimore, Atlanta, Pittsburgh, St. Louis, and Minneapolis-St. Paul SMSAs, each with a population over 2 million, had 3 percent or fewer of the adult labor force born outside the United States. And 44 of 79 SMSAs with populations over 500,000 had fewer than 5 percent of the adult labor force born outside the United States; 26 had fewer than 3 percent born outside the United States. In Canada, by contrast, only one of nine Census Metropolitan Areas with a population greater than 500,000 had fewer than 15 percent of the adult labor force born outside Canada (1981 Public Use Sample Tape, 2 percent individual file).

7 *Newsweek*, August 9, 1993, 19; the poll was conducted in July.

and the minorities in the two countries. Not all cross-border comparisons are, however, relevant to this purpose. To be relevant, a comparison must use specific minority groups whose communities in
Canada and the United States have similar cultural characteristics
and similar histories. An intriguing comparison of patterns of residential concentration in Canada and the United States (Fong 1991)
has shown that, in the case of blacks, the degree of concentration is
much higher in the United States than it is in Canada, whereas in the
case of Asians, there is little difference between the two countries.
This finding is interesting because the Asian communities in the two
countries have had very similar histories. Detailed examination of
relevant comparisons can reveal much about relations between groups
in each country. It can expose the actual patterns of cultural retention
and social differences in the discrimination that underlie the somewhat different historical and demographic backgrounds of the two
countries.

2. *Canadian governments have adopted "multicultural" policies and US
governments have not.* Does this difference between the two countries
translate into a significant difference in their treatment of minorities?
Government policies that favor cultural diversity, by encouraging
greater tolerance or providing resources for cultural maintenance,
may produce results different from those that would occur in their
absence. It is uncertain, however, whether such results, if they exist
at all, significantly counterbalance the innumerable day-to-day pressures that encourage assimilation.

Whatever the practical effect of Canada's official "multiculturalism," its mere existence would seem to reflect a commitment to
cultural diversity, at the level of public discourse, that is absent in
the United States. Similarly, the traditional emphasis in American
discourse on the term "melting pot" suggests a commitment to
cultural assimilation that is absent in Canada.

In fact, the difference in terminology may not really bear much
emphasis. It is true that, in the United States, the metaphor of the
melting pot, as a synonym for immigrant assimilation, has had a long

history. The melting pot motif was especially prominent during the early decades of this century, a period in which a policy of open immigration yielded to a quota system that favored northern Europeans. During the same period, however, Canada too displayed a strong preference, backed by legislation, for immigrants whose culture was like that of the Anglo-Saxon majority — a clear indication of a desire to minimize cultural diversity. Nor were Canadian discussions of immigration less assimilationist than their American counterparts. To cite just one example, *Strangers within Our Gates*, (Woodsworth [1909] 1972), an early twentieth-century commentary on immigration, advocated rapid assimilation of immigrants. Over time, both Canada and the United States have moved toward a greater emphasis on cultural pluralism, and in recent decades observers in both countries have shown an increasing willingness to regard cultural diversity as a positive social force. Canada has not been notably in advance of the United States in this respect: "multiculturalism" as official policy in Canada is less than 30 years old and, as we have noted, the policy has recently attracted criticism. The fact is that, in *both* Canada and the United States, the public discourse on immigration reflects *both* a tolerance for diversity and a bias toward assimilation.

The terms "melting pot" and "multiculturalism" themselves participate in this ambiguity. The melting pot, as Americans use the term, is not always a vessel in which all minorities are assimilated to the majority. Often, it is simply a social arena in which there are diverse contacts among groups. This usage emphasizes intercultural influences and economic mobility rather than the elimination of ethnic vestiges. Nor does Canada's official multiculturalism reflect only a desire to ensure that minorities retain their cultural identities. Politically, it is a byproduct of the French-English conflict. Some ethnic minorities saw the appointment in 1963 of the Royal Commission on Bilingualism and Biculturalism as a step toward the establishment of official cultures in Canada; the "multiculturalism" movement was an effort to forestall this possibility. No such issue arose in the United States.

There is, then, reason to doubt whether the historical identification of the term "melting pot" with the United States and the term "multiculturalism" with Canada reflects real differences in intergroup relations in the two countries. In addition, even if comparative studies show that assimilationist pressures have been stronger in the United States, it does not follow that assimilation occurs more frequently in that country. Pressure to assimilate and assimilation are distinct social variables. One refers to the behavior of the dominant group, the other to the response of the minority groups. An inverse relation between the two variables is possible; that is, pressure to assimilate might bring about minority community maintenance as a defensive response. To the extent that this is the case, tolerance for diversity will actually facilitate assimilation. Any comparison of societies should examine majority-group behavior and minority-group behavior separately.

3. *The United States has a history of serious racial conflict and Canada does not.* Consequently, obstacles to intergroup understanding may exist in the United States that do not exist, at least to the same extent, in Canada.

Episodes of racial conflict in recent decades have focused world attention on the problem of race relations in the United States. Many Canadians seem to assume that the existence of this problem indicates not only that racial tensions in the United States are deeply entrenched, but that Americans are more likely than Canadians are to practice racial discrimination — that existing racial conflicts may not only reflect, but also reinforce, the potential for discrimination. Thus a poll conducted in 1986 found that 72 percent of Canadians believe that Canadians show more racial tolerance than Americans do (*Globe and Mail*, May 6, 1986, p. A7). In addition, it is worth noting the following observation by Gordon Fairweather, the former chief commissioner of the Canadian Human Rights Commission and more recently the chairman of the Immigration and Refugee Board:

> Discrimination against blacks in the United States, another
> country of immigrants, has unique historical roots. No region of

Canada has [had] an economy dependent on the labour of slaves on the scale of the United States. For this reason, the past and present experiences of the black community in the United States may not be directly useful in interpreting the present situation of multiplicity of racial and ethnic groups in Canada. (Canadian Human Rights Commission 1986, 3.)

The implication is that the United States' history of racial polarization may work to the disadvantage of racial-minority immigrants in the United States. Since Canada lacks such a history, the prospects for immigrants in Canada are better.

In fact, racial discrimination in the United States may have less to do with the country's history of racial conflict than with other, less uniquely "American" factors. According to the "perceived threat" hypothesis, discrimination against a minority group increases with the size of the group. This line of reasoning has been examined in many US sociological studies, some of which suggest that discrimination against blacks in the United States may indeed be related to the fact that American blacks are a large group (Tienda and Lii 1987). Other studies suggest that antagonism between whites and blacks in the United States may be attributable in part to competition between racial groups in racially split labor markets (Bonacich 1972; also see Olzak 1983; and Olzak and Nagel 1986). Disadvantaged whites may feel greater hostility than other whites toward blacks because they stand in a competitive social and economic relation with blacks. On the other hand, numbers may also work to the advantage of minority groups, by causing at least a minimum overflow into high-status occupations, or by increasing political clout and bargaining power.

What is needed is direct evidence of how Canadians and Americans respond to comparable interracial situations. When the comparison involves racial minorities other than blacks, the differences do not seem as striking as the similarities. The treatment in Canada of native peoples, for example, has been the target of criticism both at home and abroad and is not obviously superior to American treatment of native Americans. The treatment in the nineteenth century of Chinese railway construction workers, the imposition well into the present century of severe restrictions on Asian immigration, and the denial of the franchise to some groups at certain times are other instances of hostile treatment of racial minorities in Canada (Davis and Krauter 1971; Hughes and Kallen 1974; Palmer 1982; Barrett 1987). These instances do not indicate striking US-Canadian differences in racial tolerance, which might be suggested by focusing only on black/white relations.

One might also cite the treatment of the Japanese in the United States and Canada during the Second World War. The record seems broadly similar in the two countries. Indeed, a Canadian study (Miki and Kobayashi 1991, 51) suggests that the Japanese received significantly better treatment in the United States. In Canada, Japanese property was confiscated and Japanese internees were required to pay for their own internment, barred from military service, and separated from their families; none of this occurred in the United States. After the war, moreover, the Canadian government barred the Japanese from returning to the west coast and deported some of them to Japan; this policy, which lasted until 1949, had no counterpart in the United States (see also Adachi [1976] 1991). The compensation agreement reached with the Canadian government in 1988 did not occur until after the US settlement, and it followed the US standard (Miki and Kobayashi 1991, 110, 138–139; see also Kobayashi 1992). In any case, the recent reparations may have less to do with any increase in tolerance in either country than with the rising international position of Japan.

Many Americans who do not doubt the seriousness of black grievances nevertheless point to black socio-economic and political advancement as testimony to a comparatively strong American commitment to racial justice and reform. The American ideal of equality of opportunity and the "American dream" of material success for immigrants are elements of the national mythology that are at least as important as the mosaic imagery is in Canada. The elements suggest the existence of social forces opposed to racial discrimination.

Thus, the history of racial conflict in the United States does not necessarily imply that individual Canadians are less likely to engage in racial discrimination in specific areas, such as employment or housing, than individual Americans. Nor can we assume that individual immigrants of racial minority backgrounds are less likely to be accepted by Americans into the social mainstream. No conclusions are possible in the absence of direct comparisons of attitudes toward minorities, patterns of discrimination against racial-minority immigrants, and patterns of social mobility among racial-minority immigrants.

4. *The history of French-English relations is a source of a Canadian tradition of intergroup accommodation, a tradition that affects the treatment of other groups such as immigrant minorities.* However, the view that French-English relations have been characterized by an unusual degree of accommodation may not be justified. French-English relations have always been one of the most important sources of conflict in Canada. This can hardly be doubted, given the persistent possibility over the past three decades of Quebec separation and independence. How French-English relations in Canada affect the position of minorities composed of immigrants and their descendants is a complex sociological question (see Reitz 1980a). As we have already pointed out, it was the movement by French and English elites toward the adoption of bicultural policies that prompted other ethnic groups to demand the adoption of multicultural policies. As well, the position of immigrant minorities has been one focus of French-English conflict. Although many English-Canadians have embraced multiculturalism, many French-Canadians have worried that it may serve to reduce their status in Canada to that of one minority among many. The issue has been complicated in recent years by the Quebec government's adoption of its own version of multiculturalism, which it calls a policy of "cultural convergence." Instead of encouraging the perpetuation of separate languages and cultures, the Quebec policy seeks to promote a fusion between minority and majority cultures.

The idea that English-Canadians encourage ethnic groups to retain their cultural identities as part of a strategy of domination was a key argument in John Porter's critique of Canadian society in *The Vertical Mosaic* (1965, 63–71) and in more recent essays (Porter 1975; 1979). According to Porter, English-Canadian elites adopted a colonialist national development strategy that called for immigrant minorities to retain both their traditional cultures and their traditional subordinate status. If minorities were encouraged to retain their own cultures, they would develop their own institutions and thus isolate themselves from the social and economic mainstream. Porter argues that society's institutions should not function on the basis of ethnic differentiation.

Porter's critique underscores the need to examine how the two dimensions of culture and individual opportunity are related in fact. An individual member of the majority group may favor cultural diversity provided that it does not affect mainstream social institutions. If so, the result may be minority-group marginality. Alternatively, an individual may strongly support the principle of equal treatment, regardless of culture, and yet oppose cultural pluralism. Equality of opportunity can be a strategy for assimilation.

Whether there is a conflict between the collective interests of francophones in Quebec and the interests of various minority groups, including people of British origin, is one of the issues in the constitutional debate. Should the individual rights of members of minorities in Quebec have to be subordinated to the collective interests of the francophone majority? Quebec's application of assimilationist policies to immigrants and to anglophone migrants from elsewhere in Canada has already produced tension between French-Canadians and members of those groups.

These considerations suggest that the binational structure of Canada is no guarantee of tolerance of minorities. They also suggest that an empirical comparison of the positions of minorities in Canada and minorities in the United States should examine possible differences in the position of minorities in the different regions of the two countries. In fact, it is possible that the regional differences within Canada and the United States are more important than the aggregate differences between them. Unfortunately, because of limitations of data, it will not always be possible in this study to take regional differences into account.

5. *There are various general cultural differences between Canada and the United States that might be expected to affect the ways in which the two countries treat ethnic minorities.* Thus, Canadians, in distinguishing themselves from Americans, often cite what is referred to as Canadian "tolerance" — that is, a habit of accommodating differences and avoiding rancorous conflicts that may imply a greater willingness than most Americans display to accept minorities on their own terms. However, even if Canadians are more accommodating and less contentious than Americans, it does not necessarily follow that they are also more egalitarian. One might as easily argue that avoidance of conflict actually perpetuates inequalities, by pushing them out of sight.

Canadians and Americans may also differ in their responses to the competing claims of individual rights and collective rights. Seymour M. Lipset (1989, 152–158) has marshalled evidence to support the claim that Americans tend to value individualism, individual competition and achievement, and equality of opportunity, whereas Canadians tend to defer to elites and to value equality of result. He first advanced these hypotheses in *The First New Nation* (Lipset 1963), which traced the divergence between American and Canadian values to the founding experiences of the two countries. The United States was the product of a popular rebellion against an imperial system, a rebellion that asserted the primacy of individual rights. Canadians, both French and English, took a counterrevolutionary stance and retained their attachments to traditional institutions, which stressed the group rather than the individual.

The presence in Canada of two distinct cultural groups encouraged this emphasis on group prerogatives. Because the French were a conquered people, the British administration could not take their loyalty for granted. They were also, for a long time, more numerous than the British. The latter responded to this state of affairs by recognizing the language and religion of the French while taking care to provide protection for their own language and religion. This pragmatic recognition of collective rights was subsequently embedded in the Canadian Constitution, which stands in contrast with the US Constitution and its emphasis on individual rights (Elkins 1989).

American individualism, associated as it is with a commitment to meritocratic competition, might be expected to translate into disapproval of racial or ethnic discrimination. There is nothing automatic about this, however. Individualism includes the idea of doing as you please, an idea that might be invoked to insulate discriminatory practices from regulation. Individualism also emphasizes self-reliance, which implies an opposition to the regulation of competition in the economy. This opposition could lead to an inability or unwillingness to acknowledge discriminatory practices in employment that might undermine meritocracy. Sniderman and Hagen (1985) show that Americans' commitment to individualism and self-reliance is an important reason many of them oppose government action to assist blacks. Thus, individualist opposition to government regulation might offset individualist support for meritocracy and universal competition.

Lipset agrees, arguing as well that Canadian elitism might promote tolerance. He points to the views of the Canadian historian Kenneth McNaught (1966, 508), who, in turn, cited Tocqueville's analysis of pressures to conform — "the tyranny of the majority" — in the individualistic, egalitarian society of the United States in the 1830s (Tocqueville [1835 and 1840] 1942). McNaught suggested that elitist societies have a "tradition of eccentricity" and hence a greater tolerance for diversity than egalitarian societies do. McNaught was concerned with tolerance for socialist ideas,[8] but his theory may apply as well to tolerance for cultural differences. In addition, if it is

---

8 The question whether Canada has been more receptive to socialism than the United States is a recurrent one in the comparative analysis of North American political culture, but it is not clearly related to the question of tolerance for racial minorities. A quantitative analysis by Gibbins and Nevitte (1985) suggests that ideological polarization is greater in the United States but that the basic right- and left-wing positions in the United States are essentially the same as those in Canada.

true, as Lipset suggests, that Canadians place a greater emphasis than Americans do on equality of result, and show a greater willingness to constrain competition in order to promote this equality, then one might reasonably expect Canadians to respond more sympathetically to claims made by disadvantaged groups and to show more support for antidiscrimination measures.

Survey research that compares Canadian and American attitudes and values has not established a consistent link between individualism, achievement-orientation, or elitism and support for meritocracy, equality, or tolerance. Only a few of the studies cited by Lipset directly concerned equality values.[9] Public opinion data compiled by Hastings and Hastings (1982, 519, 520, and 525) showed that, as expected by Lipset, Canadians were more favorable to equality than Americans were and less favorable to inequality based on ability; the difference in each case was 9 percent.[10] The CARA-Gallup value studies (Lipset 1989, 157–158) also found a slightly greater US pref-

---

9 Most of the studies concerned individualism, collectivity-orientation, elitism, or achievement-orientation, and the actual results seem less conclusive than Lipset suggests. The study by Crawford and Curtis of value-orientations in two border communities focused on achievement orientation (it found a 10 percent difference favoring Lipset's hypothesis) and community participation (which was valued 23 percent more often by Americans). However, Crawford and Curtis did not find Canadians to be more traditional than Americans, or more oriented to the collectivity. A study of child-rearing values by Lambert, Hamers, and Frasure-Smith (1979) found English-Canadian parents to be more demanding than American parents but did not draw Lipset's implication of greater Canadian elitism. The studies by Pineo and Porter (1973) and by Guppy (1983–84) concerned occupational prestige. They showed slight tendencies for Canadians to give high status occupations more prestige. Pineo, in fact, stressed the lack of cross-national difference. Rokeach (1974, 162–64) found American college students to be more achievement-oriented, but not more egalitarian or individualistic. Finally, a re-analysis of cross-national data on class consciousness (Lipset 1989, 154) showed Canadians are more class-conscious, but only by about 6 to 8 percent.

10 Forty-one percent of Canadians and 32 percent of Americans agreed with a statement to the effect that liberalism produces too much emphasis on inequality and rejected a statement to the effect that people should be "given the opportunity to choose their own economic and social life according to their individual abilities."

erence for inequality on the basis of merit.[11] The effects of these differences on the position of minorities is not clear. The greater emphasis on meritocracy in the United States may translate into less discrimination and hence more tolerance, contrary to the Canadian tolerance hypothesis. On the other hand, the greater emphasis on equality in Canada may lead to higher status for minorities. In either case, the measured differences may not be large enough to constitute important sources of cross- national differences in relations among ethnic groups.[12]

The possible implications of Canadian-American differences in the value of individualism for discriminatory treatment of minorities is also suggested by theories about labor markets. Labor markets in the United States are more individualistic than their Canadian counterparts, in the sense that they are less regulated and have lower rates of unionization (Meltz 1989; Adams 1989; Bruce 1989; Kumar 1993). Labor-market theorists have debated the implications of these differences for employment discrimination, though without reaching a consensus. Theorists of segmented labor markets (see, for example, Piore 1979; Portes and Walton 1981; Castles 1989) might argue that racial-minority immigrants must suffer greater discrimination in the United States, since the disadvantaged labor market segments are larger there. On the other hand, theorists of competitive labor markets (see, for example, Becker 1964; 1971) and postindustrialism (Bell 1973) might argue that the American emphasis on open competition, skills, and technological innovation favors meritocracy and thus undermines discrimination. This was one of John Porter's principle

---

11 Respondents were presented with a story about two secretaries, one of whom is paid more but is "quicker, more efficient, and more reliable at her job." Thirty-two percent of francophone Canadians, 23 percent of anglophone Canadians, and 17 percent of Americans said it was "unfair to pay the more efficient worker at a higher rate." The difference between anglophone Canadians and Americans was only 6 percent. Americans were also 8 percent more likely than anglophone Canadians and 15 percent more likely than francophone Canadians to agree with a statement that favored freedom over the reduction of class differences.

12 A critique by Baer, Grabb, and Johnston (1990), with a reply and rejoinder by Lipset, shows the difficulty of interpreting cross-national differences in attitude-survey results.

arguments in *The Vertical Mosaic* (1965). Studies by McRoberts and Selbee (1981) and Cuneo and Curtis (1975) have found no major differences in mobility patters in the two countries that clearly arise from differences in labor market structure. However, the implications of differences in labor market structure for ethnic and racial minorities have yet to be examined empirically in a systematic way.

A recent study by Fletcher (1992) disputes the suggestion that Canadians are less achievement-oriented than Americans. Fletcher, who compares the results of his own 1987 Canadian survey with those of a 1984 US study by McClosky and Zaller, does find that more Americans than Canadians believe that, in a fair economic system, people with more ability should earn more (78 percent of Americans and 71 percent of Canadians) and that competitiveness leads to better performance (81 and 73 percent). He notes, however, that more Canadians think "it's very important to be the best at what you do" (74 percent of Canadians and 55 percent of Americans) and that the profit system teaches the value of hard work (61 and 54 percent). In Fletcher's view, these results challenge the findings of an earlier study, funded by the Canadian government and conducted by the Harvard economist Michael Porter (1991), that criticized the lack of competitiveness in the Canadian economy.

Several studies have shown that Canadians are less religious today than Americans are, despite the Canadian image of traditionalism; Canadians are also much less involved in Protestant fundamentalist movements.[13] Religion teaches one to love one's neighbor

---

13 Lipset (1989, 84–87) cites two international studies based on Gallup poll data (Gallup International Research Institute 1977; Centre for Applied Research in the Apostolate 1983) for evidence that religious beliefs are more important to Americans. Thus 56 percent of Americans but only 36 percent of Canadians say they are "very important," two-thirds of Americans but only one-half of Canadians believe that God administers rewards and punishments on the basis of our behavior and Americans lead Canadians in belief in an afterlife by 15 percentage points. The World Values survey, cited by Inglehart (1990), reports that only 45 percent of Canadians but 60 percent of Americans attend church. According to Gallup poll data assembled by Michalos (1982), most people in both countries say that they believe in God, but the Americans have a slight edge — 98 percent to 92 percent. Americans are more likely by margins ranging from 13 to 25 points...

and to do good for others, principles that might be expected to have a positive effect on attitudes toward ethnic or racial minorities. Stark and Glock (1968, 71) offer some support for this expectation: they found that people who believe it is important to adhere to these principles if one is to be saved are more likely than others to think that racial discrimination may be an obstacle to salvation.

The same writers, however, have also identified other values associated with organized religion that may have a less positive effect (Glock and Stark 1966, 135–138). They found that religious fundamentalism may diminish tolerance of ethnic cultural diversity, particularly where it is reflected in religious diversity.[14] A study conducted in Toronto in the late 1970s found that negative attitudes toward racial minorities were significantly related to religious affiliation.[15] Those who reported no religion had the least negative views; Jews, Roman Catholics, Anglicans, and members of the United Church were in an intermediate category; and Baptists, Lutherans, and Presbyterians were the most likely to express negative views of racial minorities.

Related to religion is the theme of moral conservatism generally. In a 1974 study, Arnold and Tigert found that significantly more Americans than Canadians supported the conservative position on

---

Note 13 - cont'd.

...to believe in the devil, hell, life after death, and heaven. Relatively few in either country believe in reincarnation, but Canada has the edge on that one: 26 percent of Canadians believe but only 20 percent of Americans.

14 Glock and Stark developed an index of "religious bigotry" and related it to anti-Semitism. The index included items related to the belief that only one's own religion is legitimate, belief in the strict interpretation of the Bible, belief in taking punitive action against those with different religious beliefs, and other, related beliefs. At least some of these beliefs may in fact be related to tolerance of cultural minorities.

15 See Henry (1978, 26). Henry prepared a "racism scale" based on a factor analysis of 29 items, including items that measured belief in the inferiority of certain racial groups and items that reflected negative attitudes toward minorities or social distance.

all but one of 11 issues related to popular morality.[16] Moral conservatism in the United States may limit Americans' willingness to adjust to social change in general, including changes in the country's ethnic and racial composition. Inglehart (1990, 104) finds that Canadians are more accepting of homosexuality than Americans are — 51 percent of Canadians but 65 percent of Americans say that "homosexuality can never be justified"; the difference is much greater for persons under 55.[17] Lipset (1989, 188–192) argues that the women's movement in Canada has enjoyed greater success than its counterpart in the United States and attributes this result to the lesser strength in Canada of religious-based traditional views about gender. He notes that women's participation in both higher education and the labor force has grown more rapidly in Canada, that equal rights for women are enshrined in the Canadian Constitution but not in that of the United States, and that Ontario has gone "much further than any American state in enacting legislation requiring that women receive the same pay as men for jobs of comparable skill" (Lipset 1989, 190).

---

16 The national samples analyzed by Arnold and Tigert (1974) support the view of Americans as more individualist and achievement-oriented and less financially conservative than Canadians. Americans were more likely than Canadians, however, to complain of sex and violence in the media and to call for movie censorship, fewer privileges for the young, and more discipline and hard work. Americans were more likely to agree that "you can't have respect for a girl who gets pregnant before marriage" and that "a father should be boss in the house."

17 Inglehart (1990) suggests that increasing material security in advanced industrial societies has lead to a shift from materialist to postmaterialist values and a concomitant emphasis on "belonging, self-expression, and the quality of life." In his view, postmaterialism implies a reduced need for absolute values, with the result that people "can more readily accept deviation from familiar patterns" and can "accept cultural change more readily" (Inglehart 1990, 178). This could have direct implications for tolerance of ethnic or racial diversity, and equal opportunity for culturally diverse groups. Inglehart measured postmaterialism by using an index that included items such as the importance of giving people more say in the decisions of government or at work and in the community, protecting freedom of speech, cleaning up the environment, making society less impersonal, and putting ideas ahead of money. He measured materialism by using items such as fighting inflation, maintaining economic growth and stability, building defense, maintaining order, and fighting crime. Canada ranks somewhat higher on Inglehart's postmaterialism scale than does the United States (Inglehart 1990, 58–59).

Nationalism is another cultural theme that receives more emphasis in the United States than it does in Canada. Clark (1962) argued that Canada is less nationalistic than the United States because Canadian society has encouraged the retention of diverse ethnic cultures in order to differentiate itself from American society and thus protect Canadian independence: "Efforts to check American influences in Canadian cultural life...involved the strengthening of the supports of ethnic group loyalties....Paradoxically, the security of the Canadian nation has depended upon discouraging a too strong Canadian nationalism" (p. 195). In Clark's view, then, Canadian attitudes toward cultural retention are a defensive response to the presence of a powerful neighbor. Instead of developing a competing Canadian nationalism, Canadians have chosen to fight Americanization and the lure of the American melting pot. They have preferred to rely on existing loyalties rather than risk the consequences of replacing them with a weak Canadian identity.

Parameters for an Empirical Study of Differences between Canada and the United States

These ideas about differences between the two countries have fostered an imagery of a Canadian mosaic and an American melting pot that may, in fact, be illusory. Does the imagery fit the reality? The purpose of our study is to review the existing evidence on the quality of relations among ethnic, racial, and cultural groups in Canada and the United States.

Accommodations among ethnic groups are the result of "social negotiations" that take place over time. Members of different groups attempt to negotiate the most advantageous place for themselves in the social structure. The power relationships among the groups, however, are asymmetric. Individually and collectively, the members of different ethnic groups exercise different amounts of economic, political, and social power. The question is how this unequal distribution of power affects relations among groups.

We assume that in each of the two countries there has been historically and continues to be a group (or groups) with more power than other groups to set the conditions for participation in the country's economic, political, and social institutions. The terms we use to refer to these two categories of groups vary with the context. "Dominant," "majority," "mainstream," and "receiving society" (in relation to immigrants) refer to the first category; "subordinate," "minority," "ethnic," and "immigrant" designate the second category. Each pair of terms indicates an asymmetry: dominant-subordinate; majority-minority; mainstream-ethnic; receiving society-immigrant. The expression "vertical mosaic" conveys this asymmetry. It is also embodied in "Anglo-conformity," which refers to the fact that people are expected and frequently compelled to adopt the language, ways of thinking, and mores of the English — that is, the group that, historically, has been dominant in both the United States and Canada (in a number of ways, a process of Franco-conformity can be observed in contemporary Quebec). When the term "majority" is used in this study, it refers to this historically dominant group, although it may not be dominant today in some social and institutional contexts. "Minority," on the other hand, refers to those who have been expected to or made to conform, although they may not be subject to the same pressures today.

This asymmetry is the reason we ask a different question for each of the two categories of groups about the quality of relations between them. The questions are these: First, what are the conditions set by the more powerful group or groups? Second, what is the response of the less powerful groups that, by and large, have to function within those conditions? When we enquire about the dominant group, our interest is in its stance toward minorities. When we ask about a minority, our interest is in how its members respond to the treatment they receive. As we pointed out earlier, Canadian beliefs about relations among ethnic groups refer to two distinct aspects of those relations — culture and socioeconomic opportunity. Accordingly, the basic questions must be recast for each of these two aspects. In the case of culture, the questions become the following:

- To what extent does the majority group tolerate or encourage the retention of minority-group culture and identity?
- To what extent does the minority group actually retain its own culture and group identity?

In the case of opportunity, the questions are these:

- To what extent does the majority group ensure equal opportunity, and the absence of discrimination, for minority groups in areas such as employment?
- To what extent does the minority group actually become incorporated into the social and economic mainstream?

Our main interest in this study is in aggregate differences between Canada and the United States, and we shall not attempt to test every hypothesis about these differences that we have alluded to in our discussion so far. An accurate description of the aggregate differences depends, however, on a careful consideration of a number of secondary variables. In examining the stance of the dominant group, for example, it is important to distinguish between attitudes and behavior. Attitudes, moreover, may vary with the arenas of activity to which they apply.

Our descriptions will also consider important differences within groups in each country, paying special attention to age, gender, and education. Region, too, is a significant variable, since regional variations within the two countries may be more important than the differences between them. For example, cross-national differences that are largely attributable to Quebec or the US South do not have the same significance as differences that lack a regional basis.

Differences between the two countries in race or ethnic relations may depend as well on the particular minority group in question, so the description should take account of particular relationships. It should also take account of change over time. Ethnic and race relations have changed dramatically in both Canada and the United States over the past few decades, so the description should distinguish differences between the two countries from differences related to historical changes in both countries. Finally, the involvement of government in relations among groups may also vary, independently of variations in these relations in the society at large.

The following chapters review comparative Canadian and US data on relations among ethnic and racial groups, focusing on carefully selected social indicators. We shall consider previous comparative studies and also present new analyses of data from various sources, including two cross-national *Maclean's*/Decima polls, other comparative surveys, and the Canadian and US censuses.

Most of the studies reviewed here use either census data or ethnic categories as defined in the national censuses. There are three points that the reader should bear in mind. First, these categories are based on objective criteria that may not correspond to the subjective conceptions of individuals. Second, census definitions can change over the years. Third, and most important in the present context, many groups are too small to justify the separate collection, presentation, and analysis of data for each of them. The census, therefore, combines some categories into more inclusive ones, such as "non-whites," "blacks," "European," "non-European," and "British Isles origins." It would cramp the style of the book enormously to repeat these cautions each time one of these categories was used. We have made an effort to avoid ambiguous designations, but this has not always been possible.

Chapter 2

Attitudes toward the
Retention of Minority Cultures

Do Canadians support the idea of cultural pluralism more than Americans do? Although there have been several surveys of relevant Canadian opinion in recent decades, we have found only one survey of American opinion — and it is a survey that was conducted in both countries by a Canadian organization, Decima Research Ltd. The failure of US polling organizations to address the issue of cultural diversity suggests that there is a greater preoccupation with the issue — at least among those who sponsor surveys — in Canada than there is south of the border. One reason this is so, no doubt, is the fact that Canadian governments actively encourage cultural diversity, whereas in the United States a policy of *laissez-faire* seems to prevail.

A Canada-United States Comparison

Decima Research, sponsored by *Maclean's* magazine, carried out its survey in 1989.[1] One of the questions asked of the 1,000 Canadians and 1,000 Americans in the poll was the following: "What do you think is better for [Canada/the United States], for new immigrants to be encouraged to maintain their distinct culture and ways, or to change their distinct culture and ways to blend with the larger society?"[2] Two overall results are noteworthy. First, in both countries

---

1 *Maclean's* published the results of the poll in July 1989. "The results are considered accurate to within 3.3 percentage points 19 times out of 20" (*Maclean's* 1989, 48).

2 The alternative was rotated in the administration of the survey.

less than a majority of the respondents favored cultural retention. Second, the results are the reverse of what one would have expected, given the prevailing Canadian system of belief: 47 percent of the Americans, but only 34 percent of the Canadians, favored the maintenance of "distinct cultures and ways."

This difference should be considered in the context of other possible differences. The observed discrepancy in attitudes toward cultural maintenance may be attributable to differences between the two populations in variables such as education, age, ethnic origin, ideas about the ways individuals are expected to relate to the social order, and views about the integration of the two countries. Even though the Decima survey was not designed for the purpose of studying attitudes toward cultural maintenance, it offers some opportunities for our analysis.

Demographic Composition

The difference between Americans and Canadians in their level of support for minority cultural maintenance holds for most categories of gender, age, and education. There are, however, variations in the size of the difference. It is about the same among men (13 percent) as it is among women (11 percent). It is more pronounced among those under 30 years of age (18 percent) and those aged 30 to 39 (19 percent) than it is among those aged 40 to 59 (9 percent) and those aged 60 and over (3 percent). It is small among university graduates (4 percent) but substantial among those with other kinds of postsecondary education (16 percent). The proportion of university graduates is much larger in the United States (24 percent) than it is in Canada (14 percent), so in spite of the smallness of the difference in this case, US university graduates account for a significant share of the overall difference. In short, one can attribute most of the difference between the two countries to those under 40 years of age and those with some postsecondary (but not university) education.

The two countries differ significantly in ethnocultural and racial composition. In the United States, the pivotal difference is racial;

in Canada, it is linguistic. The foreign-born population is larger in Canada — 16 percent in 1991 — than it is in the United States — 8 percent in 1990. The Decima survey sorted its respondents into the following categories: "British/Irish," "French," "other European," "Black," and "other origins."[3] The proportion of people of "British/ Irish" origin is larger in Canada, and the proportion of people of "other European" origins is larger in the United States.

In all of the ethnocultural and racial categories, more Americans than Canadians favor cultural maintenance. But some categories contribute more than others to the difference between the two countries. For instance, among respondents of "British/Irish" origin, the difference is only 6 percent; among respondents of "other European" origins, it is 12 percent. The latter difference's contribution to the overall difference is increased by the fact that people of "other European" origins account for 45 percent of the US population but only 23 percent of the Canadian population. The point is not that support for cultural maintenance among those of "other European" origins is particularly high in the United States but that it is surprisingly low in Canada: for Americans in this category, the figure is 47 percent; for Canadians, 33 percent. No other ethnocultural category in Canada shows less support for multiculturalism, and yet initially at least multiculturalism was addressed precisely to that segment of the Canadian population.

The relatively low degree of support for minority cultural maintenance (33 percent) among the "French" in Canada is not surprising, given the strong linguistic and cultural initiatives of the Quebec government in recent decades — in particular, those aimed at integrating immigrants into the francophone community. French-Canadians constitute a significant proportion of the sample, so their contribution to the overall difference between the two countries is substantial.

---

3 Because the number of "French" respondents in the United States is small, this group is included in the "other European" category.

Table 1: *Percentages Favoring Immigrant Cultural Maintenance in Canada and the United States, 1989*

| | Canada | | | | United States | |
| | Non-French | | French | | | |
	(%)	*(number)*	*(%)*	*(number)*	*(%)*	*(number)*
Age						
Under 30	49	182	33	45	62	245
30–39	38	167	39	46	56	250
40–59	34	216	31	64	41	280
60 and over	26	96	29	38	30	198
Education						
Elementary and some high school	28	177	27	64	38	108
High school	39	196	36	45	43	309
Some postsecondary	33	136	39	43	54	317
University	50	100	38	26	51	231

Source: Maclean's/Decima survey 1989; see ch. 2, note 1.

The desire to integrate immigrants into the francophone majority is a relatively recent phenomenon in Quebec. It would, accordingly, occur more frequently among the young and perhaps among the better-educated as well. Therefore, the low support in Quebec for cultural maintenance should be concentrated among the younger and better-educated segments of the Quebec francophone population. In fact, as Table 1 shows, it is only among those under 30 years of age that French-Canadians and other Canadians differ in their attitudes toward minority cultural maintenance: 33 percent of French-Canadians under 30 but 49 percent of other Canadians under 30 favor it. For groups over age 30, the difference between French-Canadians and other Canadians is negligible. Finally, although support for multiculturalism varies markedly by age group in the United States and among the non-French in Canada, there is not much variation by age group among French-Canadians.

A similar pattern appears when education is the variable. Table 1 shows that well-educated Americans and the non-French in Canada do not differ in their degree of support for cultural maintenance; the figure is about 50 percent in each case. It is only 38 percent, however, among university-educated French-Canadians, though this result is based on a small number of cases.

Another noteworthy finding is that university graduates of "British/Irish" origin constitute the only category in which Canadians are more supportive of minority cultural maintenance than Americans are; the proportions are 54 and 42 percent. It is also the only category, among the 12 categories of education and ethnicity combined, in which the percentage of support exceeds 50 percent. Support for minority cultural maintenance in this social category may reflect a spirit of noblesse oblige; or it may be that Canadians in this category value cultural diversity in itself or as something that distinguishes Canada from the United States. The available data do not permit an exploration of these and other interpretations.

The two remaining categories are "Black"[4] and "other origins" — that is, other non-European origins. In both categories, contrary to expectation, support for cultural maintenance is stronger in the United States than it is in Canada. Among non-Europeans other than blacks, the level of support is 57 percent in the United States and 50 percent in Canada. The difference is larger among blacks: in the United States, 61 percent of blacks support cultural maintenance; in Canada, 42 percent. This disparity contributes significantly to the overall difference between the two countries, since blacks constitute 10 percent of the US sample but only 1 percent of the Canadian sample. Thus, the low support among French-Canadians and "other Europeans" in Canada and the strong support among blacks in the United States account for much of the overall difference — but not

---

4 Whether one should regard the category "Black" in the survey as an ethnic category or as a broader category that includes several ethnic groups — as the "White" category does — is an important question that cannot be answered on the basis of the survey data.

for all of it, since, as we noted earlier, support is stronger in the United States in *all* ethnocultural and racial categories.

Ideological Orientations

Attitudes toward cultural maintenance may have their basis in larger systems of ideas. Accordingly, ideological differences may account for the fact that support for cultural maintenance is stronger in the United States. The Decima survey provides data relevant to two ideological domains: "individualism" and attitudes about social rights.

The greater support for cultural maintenance in the United States may be attributable in part to a greater adherence to individualism in that country. The American emphasis on "life, liberty, and the pursuit of happiness," which presupposes individual autonomy, may lead to support for the idea that people should be encouraged to do as they wish in all aspects of social life. In contrast, an emphasis on "peace, order, and good government," which some observers have identified as an aspect of the prevailing cultural orientation in Canada, may lead people to value a certain degree of cultural conformity.

The Decima survey asked respondents: "Which *one* of these words, in your view, best describes the ideal Canadian/American?" (*Maclean's* 1989, 49). Since the question is about an *ideal* trait, the responses to it can be taken, to a certain extent, as an expression of ideological orientation. Four epithets in the list are relevant in the present context: "aggressive," "independent-minded," "peaceful," and "tolerant."[5] The first two can be associated with the ideology of individualism, whereas "peaceful" suggests a preference for social order. "Tolerant" is somewhat ambiguous, since tolerance is consistent with both individualism and a peaceful social order.

The survey results show that the selection of ideal traits is consistent with what is said to characterize American and Canadian

---

5 We have omitted two other words: "sexy" and "clean," since only 1 percent of the respondents in both countries selected the former and only 3 percent selected the latter.

cultural orientations. More Americans than Canadians chose "aggressive" and "independent-minded"; the differences were, respectively, 9 percent and 25 percent. More Canadians than Americans chose "peaceful" and "tolerant"; in this case the respective differences were 14 percent and 17 percent. The results also show that American and Canadian respondents were more likely to differ about minority cultural maintenance if they chose one of the individualistic traits rather than one of the other options. Thus, the difference was 16 percent if the choice was "aggressive" and 14 percent if it was "independent-minded" but only 8 percent if the choice was "peaceful" and 7 percent if it was "tolerant." These figures suggest that, in the United States, support for the ideal of individualism is positively related to support for cultural maintenance, whereas in Canada, it is unrelated.

If support for minority cultural maintenance were associated with support for social rights, then one would expect support for cultural maintenance to be greater in Canada than in the United States. The Decima survey shows that Canadians are more likely than Americans to favor "the right to a publicly funded health care system available to all regardless of financial situation" (71 percent of Canadians and 52 percent of Americans) and "the right of every individual to be guaranteed a minimum income" (62 percent and 51 percent).[6]

It is true, in both countries, that those who favor such absolute rights are more likely to favor minority cultural maintenance than those who do not. However, both Canadians who favor social rights and those who do not show less support for cultural maintenance than the corresponding groups of Americans.

Attitudes toward the Integration of the Two Countries

Part of the public legitimation of the maintenance of minority cultures in Canada has been that it contributes to the distinctiveness of

---

6 For "the right to child care, available to everyone who wants it," the figures were 50 percent and 46 percent.

Canada *vis-à-vis* the United States; that it is an element of a distinctive Canadian identity. To what extent does this consideration underlie the support for minority cultural maintenance in Canada?

The survey asked respondents their views about "Canada becoming the 51st state of the United States with full congressional representation and rights of American citizenship," the "two countries adopting a common currency in money between Canada and the United States," and the "two countries adopting common and identical policy on all matters relating to defence and foreign affairs" (*Maclean's* 1989, 49–50).

Of course, although these questions may provide a measure of a kind for Canadian nationalism, they do not provide one for American nationalism. The United States has been a "significant other" in the shaping of Canadian nationalism, but Canada is not an important factor in the definition of American nationalism. Because of the differences in the size and power of the two countries, Canadians and Americans are likely to have different perceptions of what the gains and losses brought by integration would be. Thus, the meaning of the questions for Canadians is no doubt different from their meaning for Americans. In addition, the questions do not provide a measure of Quebec nationalism. Nevertheless, they do give an indication of the desire for distinctiveness.

The data show, first, that Canadians tend to oppose and Americans tend to favor integration of the two countries on all three counts: 86 percent of Canadians oppose Canada's becoming a fifty-first state, 50 percent oppose a common currency, and 61 percent oppose the adoption of common defense and a common foreign policy. In contrast, 67, 76, and 76 percent of Americans favor the three measures.

Second, as expected, Canadians who strongly oppose integration with the United States are about 20 percent more likely than those who strongly approve of it to favor minority cultural maintenance; this holds for each of the three items. Among Americans, the pattern is not clear. Those who strongly oppose integration fall between those who simply oppose it and those who favor it in their attitude toward cultural maintenance. This result is difficult to interpret. In any case, it is based on small numbers in some of the response categories.

Overall, those who favor distinctiveness and autonomy for the two countries are more likely than those who favor integration to support the distinctiveness of minority cultures. Thus, there is a sort of consistency in people's thinking, in both countries, about the two types of distinctiveness, although the pattern is less ambiguous in the Canadian sample. But whatever their views on national distinctiveness and autonomy, Americans are more likely than Canadians to favor minority cultural maintenance.

Because of the possibility that French-Canadians and other Canadians would attach different meanings to the questions, separate tabulations were made for the two groups. The results show that, among French-Canadians, there is virtually no relationship between support for national autonomy and support for minority cultural maintenance. Among other Canadians, however, the relationship is fairly strong: 47 percent of those who strongly oppose integration but only 21 percent of those who support it favor minority cultural maintenance. To the extent that each of the two collectivities endorses multiculturalism, it appears to be part of a different ideological system. For the non-French, it may be, for instance, an element defining the national identity; for the French, it may be an approach to the integration of immigrants into the French community in Quebec.

The Meaning of Cultural Retention in the Two Countries

It is possible that Canadians and Americans respond differently to questions about cultural retention in part because they think about the subject in somewhat different terms. When Canadians are asked about minority cultural maintenance, they may tend to think of government intervention in this area and to place the issue in the larger context of government activity in relation to ethnicity, language, and "national unity." Americans, on the other hand, may tend to think of cultural maintenance in relation to certain social norms or expectations, such as those that pertain to individual autonomy and self-expression.

Unfortunately, a lack of relevant data makes it impossible to explore this hypothesis. Some survey results on the Canadian side, however, suggest that it is not entirely unreasonable. A 1986 survey showed support for the government policy of multiculturalism: 59 percent did not agree that "Canada's policy promoting multiculturalism is a mistake" (Ponting 1986). On the other hand, since there was no question in the survey about the perceived objective of the policy, it is not clear what the respondents disagreed with. However, a 1974 study is suggestive in this regard (Berry, Kalin, and Taylor 1977). It asked respondents whether the Canadian policy consisted of encouraging immigrants to give up their old customs, allowing them to maintain their customs, or encouraging them to maintain their customs. Only 26 percent of the respondents said that the purpose of the policy was to encourage cultural maintenance. Sixty percent thought the policy was permissive rather than supportive, and 13 percent thought it was assimilationist (Berry, Kalin, and Taylor 1977, 142–143). Thus, Canadians may see a role for government, but a passive role rather than an active one. Clearly, more research is needed on this matter.

Studies in Canada

Some results of other studies carried out in Canada alone are worth examining, even though no comparable results are available for the United States. The following statement, for instance, appeared in surveys carried out in 1974 and 1991: "People who come to Canada should change their behaviour to be more like us."[7] In 1974, 50 per-

---

7 The wording of the statement was the same in the two surveys. Berry, Kalin, and Taylor (1977, 141) discuss the 1974 survey. The 1991 survey, carried out by Angus Reid Group Inc. (1991) included 3,325 respondents. We are grateful to Multiculturalism and Citizenship Canada for making the 1991 data available to us (dataset SSC/MUL-050-3343 in the federal collection). The interpretations of the data are those of the authors and not of Multiculturalism and Citizenship Canada.

cent of the respondents agreed with the statement; in 1991, 46 percent. The smallness of the change is probably attributable to the increase in the proportion of the population with university education, from 4.8 percent in 1974 to 11.4 percent in 1991. Adjusting for education almost equalizes the two results.

These findings are consistent with those presented earlier: they suggest that Canadians are as much assimilationists as they are pluralists. On the other hand, the similarity of the 1974 results and the 1991 results calls into question Lipset's (1989, 187) suggestion that the increased ethnic and racial heterogeneity of immigration in Canada in recent years has produced a backlash against the mosaic concept. The backlash hypothesis is further weakened by the fact that the proportion of respondents who agreed with the statement did not vary much, in either year, across ethnic identifications. In 1974, the scores for Anglo-Celtic, French, anglophone "other ethnic," and francophone "other ethnic" respondents were, respectively, 4.0, 5.1, 4.1, and 4.6.[8] The scores were higher for respondents of French origin but did not vary greatly among those in other ethnic categories. The same pattern of differences among ethnic categories prevailed in 1991: 54 percent of French-origin respondents and 44 percent of those in the other three ethnic categories agreed with the statement.

If there is a backlash, perhaps it is directed not against immigration in general or against the mosaic concept as such, but rather against nonwhite immigration and the notion of a multiracial society. However, a survey of seven Toronto ethnic minorities in the late 1970s produced some evidence that tells against this possibility. A majority of the respondents in six of the seven groups agreed that "immigrants and members of ethnic minorities should try to blend into Canadian society and not form ethnic communities." The six groups included two nonwhite groups, Chinese and West Indians,

---

8 Berry, Kalin, and Taylor 1977, 154. The study presents scores rather than percentages. The scores were obtained by assigning the following point values to the responses to the statement: disagree, 1–3; neutral, 4; and agree, 5–7. The point value varied with the degree of agreement or disagreement. The numbers given here are averages of the scores for the various ethnocultural categories.

for whom the percentages were 62 and 76, respectively (Breton et al. 1990, 215). Of course, different groups might agree with such a statement for different reasons. The backlash hypothesis may have some validity, but other factors seem to be at work as well.

Other results from the 1974 and 1991 surveys suggest that Canadians tend to favor cultural maintenance. In 1974, 64 percent agreed that "it would be good to see that all the ethnic groups in Canada retain their cultures." Also, 47 percent in 1974 and 41 percent in 1991 did not agree that "the unity of this country is weakened by ethnic groups sticking to their old ways" — again, the lower percentage in 1991 is attributable to the large number of highly educated respondents in the sample.[9]

Surveys have explored the question of private versus public manifestations of ethnic cultures. In the 1974 survey, 49 percent of the respondents agreed that members of ethnic groups who "want to keep their own culture" should "keep it to themselves and not bother other people in the country." A 1986 survey asked the respondents whether they agreed with the statement "if members of ethnic groups want to keep their own culture, they should keep it to themselves and not display it publicly"; 34 percent agreed (Ponting 1986).[10] These results suggest that many Canadians support cultural maintenance provided that it "fits" well with the ways of other groups. If minority culture is likely to interfere with mainstream society, it should remain private. These Canadians do not endorse assimilation but neither do they endorse outright pluralism. In other words, they present ethnic minorities with a twofold expectation — an expectation perhaps best captured by the term "integration."

Summary

Cultural maintenance appears to be an issue of public concern in Canada but not in the United States. Indeed, although questions

---

9 The wording of the statement was the same in the two surveys.

10 We are grateful to Professor Rick Ponting for these data. His study used a national sample of 1,834 respondents.

about cultural maintenance have found their way into several Canadian surveys over the past 15 years or so, we could find only one US survey that addressed the issue — and it was carried out by a Canadian organization!

There are several reasons minority cultural maintenance is a public issue in Canada. One is quite simply the fact that the Canadian government has made it so. It has introduced an explicit policy of minority cultural maintenance, launched a series of programs intended to promote this policy, and, recently, established a special government department to oversee the programs. Another is the fact that the proportion of foreign-born persons in the population is twice as large in Canada as it is in the United States. Still another reason is the long history of tension between English and French-Canadians — a history that raises the question of what place other ethnic groups are to have in any accommodation between them. A specific issue in this context is the demographic balance between the two linguistic groups. Because of the low birth rate among francophones in Quebec in recent decades and because immigrants have traditionally integrated into the anglophone collectivity, French-Canadians have been increasingly concerned to integrate immigrants into their linguistic community. The question of cultural retention by non-French, non-English minorities probably has a different meaning among French-speaking Canadians than it has among English-speaking Canadians, who can take it for granted that immigrants will sooner or later adopt English as their main language.

The survey that Decima Research carried out simultaneously in Canada and the United States contradicted the view of Canada *vis-à-vis* the United States that Canadians frequently proclaim. It found that Americans were significantly more likely to declare themselves in favor of minority cultural maintenance than Canadians were. This was the case for almost all categories of gender, age, education, and ethnicity, although the difference between the two countries was not the same for all categories. The difference was greatest among the young and among respondents with some post-secondary education (but not university graduates). It was also fairly

pronounced, surprisingly, among minorities of European origin —
that is, those who are supposed to be behind the origin of the
multiculturalism movement in Canada and are, presumably, its
major beneficiaries. In fact, the category in which support for minority cultural maintenance is strongest is university graduates of British origin; it is the one category in which a majority of respondents
support minority cultural maintenance and in which support is
higher in Canada than it is in the United States. For this category of
Canadians, multiculturalism may give substance to their nationalism. Specifically, it would be an element that distinguishes Canada
from the United States, a symbol of Canada's cultural sovereignty.

The somewhat surprising outcome of the survey results for the
two countries may mean that Canadians are becoming more assimilationist than they were in the past. There is other evidence that
suggests such a trend. The evidence is, however, somewhat ambiguous: what the various survey results seem to indicate is that Canadians are ambivalent about minority cultural maintenance. This
ambivalence may arise from uncertainty generated by the changes
we discussed above.

The difference in the degree of support for minority cultural
maintenance in Canada and the United States may also arise because
cultural maintenance is interpreted differently in the two socio-
political contexts. Americans seem to associate it somewhat with the
ideology of individualism, self-fulfilment, and free expression, whereas
Canadians seem to associate it with government policies and programs and bureaucratic structures. Perhaps the negative views of
minority cultural maintenance have more to do with government
intervention in this domain than with minority cultures as such.

In any case, the survey results presented here *do not* support the
notion that Canada is a society that values and encourages cultural
diversity more than does the United States.

Chapter 3

The Extent of
Cultural Retention

The view of Canadian society as a cultural mosaic implies that, in Canada, ethnic minorities are subject to relatively little pressure to assimilate; that they are even encouraged to maintain their identities and cultures. By contrast, the image of American society as a melting pot implies that, in the United States, minorities are expected to abandon their cultures and the ethnic component of their social identities. To what extent do these images of the two societies correspond to actual patterns of social identity and behavior? Do ethnic minorities in Canada maintain their identities and cultures over generations to a greater extent than do their counterparts in the United States?

This chapter examines evidence related to five dimensions of the phenomenon: (1) the salience of ethnicity for individuals, (2) intermarriage, (3) multiple origins or mixed ancestry, (4) linguistic retention, and (5) ethnic social interaction and activities. We selected these dimensions not only because they are relevant, but also because some more or less comparable research results are available for the two countries.

In considering the evidence, one must take into account the generational composition of ethnic groups of European origin in the two countries. In the United States, a majority of the members of those groups are at least third-generation Americans. Lieberson and Waters (1988, 45) report on 13 groups. In all except one, the proportion of members in this category is at least 60 percent; in nine, it is over 80 percent. In addition, "some 57 percent of the entire US population is at least fourth generation" (Lieberson 1985, 175). In Canada, by contrast, only members of the British Isles and French groups are more likely than not to be at least third-generation Canadians, and only among the French is the proportion of people in this category more than 80 percent (Richmond and Kalbach 1980, 148).[1] Another way of describing the difference is to say that the "majority" and "minority" groups do not differ markedly in their generational composition in the United States but do differ markedly in Canada.

The Salience of Ethnicity

How much importance do members of ethnic minorities give to their ethnic background? Is it a more significant component of social identities among Canadians than it is among Americans? We found evidence on three manifestations of the salience of ethnicity: knowledge of one's ancestry, ethnic identification, and the subjective importance attached to one's ethnicity.

Knowledge of One's Ancestry

People who know little about their ancestry probably consider their ethnic background to be of little importance. The lack of knowledge may be a consequence of mixed ancestry, or it may be attributable simply to poor information. In a survey, of course, a declared lack of knowledge might express respondents' unwillingness, rather than their inability, to discuss their background.

In Canada, most studies seem to find a way of classifying individuals into a particular ethnic category. In many, the "ethnic origin" variable does not include the categories "unknown" or "not

---

1 In the Richmond and Kalbach study of Canadian census data, "British" includes English, Irish, and Scottish, and "Scandinavian" includes Swedish, Norwegian, and Danish. The Lieberson and Waters study of US data reports these groups separately.

reported." An exception is the Ethnic Relations Study carried out in 1965 for the Royal Commission on Bilingualism and Biculturalism. In that study, 9 percent of the respondents did not know their ancestry or did not respond to the question.

The census data are not very helpful either. In 1961, the following procedure was given to enumerators to help them deal with people who reported that their ancestry was "Canadian," "American," or "unknown":

> Since this question refers to the time when the person or his ancestors came to this continent, the answer should refer to the ethnic groups or cultures of the old world. However, if, in spite of this explanation, the person insists that his ethnic or cultural group is "Canadian" or "U.S.A.," enter his reply in the write-in space. If the person really does not know what to reply to this question, enter "unknown." (Halli, Trovato, and Driedger 1990, 447–448.)

In 1971, the instruction was to record the latter responses in the space provided for "other". The manuals for 1981 and 1986 omitted the details about the way to deal with those who insisted that they were Canadian or American or that they did not know (Halli, Trovato, and Driedger 1990, 445–451). In any case, virtually all Canadians are assigned an ethnic origin: in 1981, about 0.5 percent were classified as "other." In 1991, the percentage was 2.9, almost all of whom — 2.8 percent — declared themselves to be "Canadian."[2]

In the United States, about 10 percent fall into the "unknown" category. Over several years, the National Opinion Research Center–General Social Survey asked respondents which countries or parts of the world their ancestors came from. In the pooled sample for the period 1972 to 1977, 8.6 percent of whites (that is, 7,983 respondents) could not name a country (Smith 1984, 85); this was also true of 10 percent of whites (3,358 respondents) in the pooled samples for 1977 to 1980 (Alba and Chamlin 1983, 241). To a subjective question

---

2 See Pryor et al. (1992) for a discussion of the issues involved in measuring ethnicity in the 1991 Canadian census.

about ethnicity in the Michigan Election Study, 9.1 percent (2,397), 10 percent (1,404), and 11.8 percent (1,954) in 1972, 1974, and 1976, respectively, declared that they did not know. In the Current Population Survey of 1972, 8.6 percent (204,840) also said they did not know their origin or descent (Smith 1984, 82–83). Alba (1990, 43) found that in the capital region of New York State (Albany and its environs) "about 15 percent of native-born whites" (460 respondents) "have some degree of uncertainty about their background."

The difference between the proportion of Canadians who declare that they do not know their ancestry and the proportion of Americans may be attributable, as noted above, to the way the information is obtained. But it may also be a result of the difference in the generational composition of ethnic groups in Canada and the United States. For instance, Lieberson (1985, 175) points out that,

> among "Unhyphenated whites" (those unable to name any ancestral country or choosing "American"), 97 percent were of at least fourth-generation ancestry. Thus Unhyphenated whites make up fully 16 percent of all Americans (and 20 percent of the non-black population) with at least four generations' residence in the country.

Although we could find no data on unhyphenated whites in Canada, the evidence on generational composition mentioned above suggests that their proportion would be quite small, except among the French.

Another manifestation of uncertainty is inconsistency between responses given at different times. This, of course, is rarely ascertained, since in order to ascertain it the researcher must match respondents in studies carried out in different years. Lieberson (1985, 174), however, reports on matched samples drawn from the US Current Population Surveys of 1971 and 1972: "in only 64.7 percent of the cases was the same ethnic response obtained from the respondent one year later."

This kind of analysis has not been carried out in Canada. However, Kralt (1980, 26–27) reports on another type of "inconsistency," found in an analysis of the 1971 census — namely, inconsistency between the paternal ancestry reported by children and the ethnic origin reported by their fathers. In 11 percent of families with children, at least one child cited an ethnic origin different from the origin cited by the father.[3] The inconsistency might arise from uncertainty on the child's part because of dual or multiple ancestries. In some cases, it might be the result of circumstances such as adoption or divorce followed by remarriage.

It is difficult to say, given the available evidence, whether Canadians are more or less likely than Americans to be familiar with their ethnic ancestry. In Canadian studies, virtually all respondents are classified in some ethnic category. What is not clear, however, is whether this is a genuine finding or simply a result of the way in which the data are collected. If it is genuine, then presumably the level of awareness of ethnic ancestry is higher in Canada than it is in the United States. This higher awareness, if it exists, may be attributable to the fact that, in Canada, issues pertaining to ethnicity (and language) have been part of the public debate for several years, whereas in the United States, racial issues are the prime focus of public attention.

Ethnic Identification

What do people say when they are asked to define or describe their ethnicity or their ethnic identity? Generally, they give one of the following types of responses: an ethnic origin, more than one origin, a hyphenated identification (such as Italian-Canadian), Canadian, American, or none. The exact meaning of each such response for the individual respondent is difficult to ascertain without additional information. However, it seems clear that for those who choose "Canadian" or "American" ethnicity has a very low level of salience.

---

3 In 7.6 percent of the families, all of the children declared a different ancestry; in 3.5 percent, some declared the same ancestry, some a different one. These figures refer to a total of 360,110 families (out of 3,235,710 with children), in which there are 722,370 children (Kralt 1980, 27, note to table 1).

Table 2: *Results of Canadian
Studies of Ethnic Identification*

	Identification Categories				Number in Sample
	Ethnic	Hyphenated	Canadian	Other	
	(percentage of respondents)				
National, 1973	14	—	86	—	44,000
National, 1974	23	18	59	—	1,849
Five cities, 1973	18	46	36	—	2,433
Winnipeg and Edmonton, 1980	43	9	40	8	730
Winnipeg, 1983	48	13	36	4	520

Sources: The results of the first three studies are taken from the summary presented in Driedger, Thacker, and Currie 1982, 60. The fourth set of results is from the study conducted by Driedger, Thacker, and Currie 1982. The last set is from Goldstein and Segall 1985.

In Canada, several studies have attempted to assess the ethnic identification of individuals in the country as a whole or in one region or city. Table 2, which sets out the results of five studies, shows that the percentage of respondents who state an ethnic identification varies considerably from one study to the next: it can be as low as 14 percent and as high as 48 percent. When the ethnic and hyphenated-ethnic categories are combined, the percentage can be as high as 64 percent. One can attribute the variation from study to study, in part, to differences in the wording, timing, and location of the surveys, and in the characteristics of the samples. It may also indicate a certain fluidity or lack of robustness in the conceptions people have of their ethnic selves.

Table 2 also shows that the percentage of respondents who define their "ethnic identity" as "Canadian" also varies considerably, from 36 to 86 percent, and is frequently higher than the percentage of those who identify themselves in ethnic terms. Even if one ignores the 1973 study, in which 86 percent of the respondents identified themselves as "Canadian,"[4] the variation is considerable — from 36 to 59 percent.

A few studies provide data indicative of changes over time. In a 1973 study, the percentage of respondents who used an ethnic identification (simple or hyphenated) was 67.9 percent in the case of adult immigrants, 54.7 percent in the case of childhood immigrants, 23.9 percent in the case of second-generation respondents, and 17 percent in the case of third-generation respondents (Reitz 1980b, 131). In a study of Winnipeg and Edmonton (Driedger, Thacker, and Currie 1982), respondents were also asked to classify their mothers and fathers. In Winnipeg, 60 percent of respondents used an ethnic category, simple or hyphenated, for themselves but 78 percent did so for their fathers and mothers. In Edmonton, the corresponding figures were 45 and 67 percent.

In the United States, "there has been virtually no attention to ethnic identity, the felt significance of ethnicity" (Alba and Chamlin 1983, 241). This lack of attention may in itself indicate a low salience of ethnicity in that country. Nevertheless, some evidence is available from the studies mentioned earlier. These results are presented in Table 3. As in Canada, there is variation across studies, although the variations are not as pronounced in the United States. The proportion of those who mention a single country or nationality of origin or descent ranges from 44 to 61 percent — if one omits the Waldinger study, which does not give a percentage for the total sample. The Current Population Survey and the census, however, systematically discouraged the response "American" and accepted it "only as a response of last resort" (Lieberson 1985, 171). Thus, the percentage of respondents classified by these surveys as having identified an ethnic or national origin might have been lower had respondents been given complete freedom of response. However, the percentages in these two surveys are not much larger than those in most of the other studies summarized in Table 3.

---

4 Driedger, Thacker, and Currie (1982) argue that the wording of the question may have encouraged respondents to give the "Canadian" response.

Table 3: Results of US Studies of Ethnic Identification

Identification Category	CPS[a] 1972	CPS[a] 1979	Census 1980	Michigan Election Studies[b] 1972	Michigan Election Studies[b] 1974	Michigan Election Studies[b] 1976	NORC—GSS[d] 1972–77	NORC—GSS[d] 1977–80	Alba 1985	Waldinger Whites	Waldinger Blacks	Waldinger Hispanics
						(percentage of respondents)						
Ethnic/one country or nationality	60	44	52	61	57	54	53	48	45	47	8	52
Race or cultural group	—	—	—	—	—	—	—	—	—	5	63	70
Multiple countries or nationalities[c]	—	38	31	12	14	10	37	42	22	11	2	1
One close to	—	—	—	—	—	—	25	29	—	—	—	—
None close to	—	—	—	—	—	—	12	13	—	—	—	—
American	—	6	6	10	10	5	1	—	—	27	6	4
Other	31	—	1	9	12	8	—	—	—	7	14	19
None	—	—	—	8	10	20	—	—	33	1	2	1
Don't know/no answer	—	11	10	9	10	12	9	10	—	3	4	3
Number of respondents	205,000	217,000	226,546	2,397	1,404	1,954	7,983	3,538	460	1,935	1,935	1,935

[a] Current Population Survey.

[b] Non-blacks only.

[c] Includes both "group nationalities" (for example, central Europe) and multiple nationalities.

[d] National Opinion Research Center—General Social Survey.

Sources: Smith 1980, 82 (CPS for 1972); United States, Bureau of the Census 1983, 4 (CPS for 1979 and Census 1980); Smith 1980, 83 (Michigan Election Studies); Smith 1980, 85 (NORC—GSS results, whites only); Alba and Chamlin 1983, 241 (NORC—GSS results); Alba 1990, 53; Waldinger 1989, 61.

Although one has to be cautious, given differences in the wording of questions, in the instructions to interviewers, and in the composition of the samples, the findings examined here suggest that there is little difference between the two countries in the extent to which people are likely to identify themselves in ethnic terms. The evidence definitely does not warrant the conclusion that Canada is "multicultural" and the United States is a melting pot. If anything, they suggest that Canada is the melting pot, since the percentage of respondents who define themselves in national terms — that is, as Canadian or American — appears to be higher in Canada than it is in the United States. It must be emphasized, however, that the evidence is not entirely comparable.

The Subjective Importance of Ethnicity

A third indicator of the salience of ethnicity is the degree to which individuals consider that their ethnicity is important to them. Few studies are available for a comparison along these lines. Table 4 presents results from three Canadian studies and one US study. They suggest that Canadians tend to attach more importance to their ethnicity than Americans do. Three important qualifications must be taken into account. First, the three Canadian studies are national in scope, whereas the US study is limited to Albany, New York, and its environs and, accordingly, cannot be taken as representative of American society as a whole. Second, the data from each of the Canadian studies refer to the entire samples, whereas the data from the US study refer only to those respondents who identified with an ethnic group. Third, the questions asked to assess identification were not the same in all of the studies.[5]

The national study carried out by Ponting in 1986[6] and the 1979 Toronto Ethnic Pluralism Study (Breton et al. 1990, 115) show varia-

---

5 In the national study carried out by Ponting, the Toronto study, and the Albany study (Alba 1990), the question asked directly "how important is your ethnic or cultural background to you?"

6 The results are from tabulations supplied by Ponting.

Table 4: Results of US and Canadian Studies of the Subjective Importance of Ethnicity

	Degree of Importance					Number in Sample
	High	Quite High	Neutral	Somewhat	Not at All	
	(percentage of respondents)					
Toronto, 1979	16	25	—	34	25	2,310
Canada, 1986	29	29	—	29	12	1,834
Winnipeg, 1983[a]	49	18	14	6	13	513
Albany, 1985[b]						
Single ancestry	34		—	40	26	—[a]
Multiple ancestry	17		—	45	38	—[a]

[a] These data are for native-born whites only.

[b] Number not given, but total sample in study was 524.

Sources: Breton et al. 1990, 115 (Toronto, 1979); Ponting 1986 (Canada, 1986); Goldstein and Segall 1985, 65 (Winnipeg, 1983); Alba 1990, 68 (Albany, 1985).

tion by generation, an important factor given the difference noted earlier between the generational composition of the Canadian population and that of the US population. In the national study, 36 percent of first-generation and 58 percent of third-generation respondents of neither British nor French origin attributed little or no importance to their ethnicity. In the Albany study, among those of single ancestry, 66 percent of third-generation and 78 percent of fourth-generation respondents declared their ethnicity to be only somewhat important or not important; for those of mixed ancestry, the percentages were 79 and 91 percent. So, even among those of the third (or later) generation, the percentage who assigned little or no importance to their ethnicity was higher in the United States than it was in Canada. In the Toronto study, the figures for the first, second, and third (or later) generations were, respectively, 37, 49, and 75 percent for respondents of German, Italian, Jewish, and Ukrainian ancestry. These results are closer to the results of the Albany study, but nevertheless this comparison, too, suggests that ethnicity is more important in Canada than it is in the United States. The suggestion remains only that, however, since once again the Albany study cannot be taken as being representative of the United States.

Intermarriage

Intermarriage is an important factor in the weakening of ethnic identities. If a member of a given ethnic group marries outside the group, it is likely that his or her attachment to that group will weaken over time. If marriages outside a given ethnic group increase over time, the less coherent the ethnicity of the group is likely to become. Yet the decision to marry outside the group in the first place does not necessarily imply a weak ethnic identity. The choice between exogamy and endogamy may depend on other factors — opportunity, for example. If a group is large, its members may intermarry simply because they are likely to meet people of their own kind; it does not necessarily follow that their ethnicity is important in their choice. On the other hand, people who belong to a small ethnic group may marry outside the group even though their ethnicity matters to them, since the smallness of the group limits their opportunities within the group (Blau, Blum, and Schwartz 1982). But whatever the motive for intermarriage, the likely effect of intermarriage is to weaken the attachment to ethnicity.

The size of groups is one determinant of rates of endogamy and exogamy; the generational composition of groups is another. Indeed, studies by Richard (1991, 127–130) in Canada and by Stevens and Swicegood (1987, 78–80) in the United States have found that group size and generational status are among the most important of the factors that affect these rates, and our analysis will follow their lead.[7]

---

7 It would be preferable in comparing the two countries to use a measure of the propensity to intermarry that took into account the differences between them in group size and generational composition. Unfortunately, the Canadian and US studies use different measures of group size. For Canada, see Richard 1991; Richard forthcoming. For the United States, see Hechter 1978; Lieberson and Waters 1988.

In Canada, intermarriage has been a trend throughout the twentieth century (Richard 1991; Richard forthcoming). The percentage of exogamous husbands was 17.1 in 1871, 11.6 in 1921; 19.8 in 1951, and 27.2 in 1981. It should be noted that the 1981 figure is not strictly comparable with those for the earlier years, since it applies only to those with a single ethnic ancestry. The exclusion of those with multiple origins probably reduces the rate of exogamy.

There is a difference between native-born and foreign-born Canadians. In 1871, 16.6 percent of native-born and 18.2 percent of foreign-born husbands were exogamous. By 1981, this difference had both widened and reversed itself: 28.9 percent of native-born and 21.7 percent of foreign-born husbands were exogamous (Richard forthcoming). Reitz's (1980b, 131) analysis of the 1973 Non- Official Language Study data provides one of the few detailed generational classifications of the data. Reitz found rates of exogamy of 22 percent for adult immigrants, 59 percent for childhood immigrants, 69 percent for second-generation persons, and 85 percent for third-generation persons.[8]

Table 5 shows the percentage of endogamous native-born wives for selected groups in the two countries. Certain ethnic groups show a higher rate of endogamy in Canada (British Isles groups, French, and Dutch) and others show a higher rate in the United States (German, Italian, and Polish). In the case of the Dutch and Scandinavian groups, the rates are not markedly different. All of these results may be attributable to differences between the two countries in the size and the generational composition of each of the groups.

Indeed, given how numerous Canadians of French descent and Americans of German descent are relative to total population, the high rates of endogamy for these groups are to be expected. The fact that the rate for the British Isles groups is lower in the United States than it is in Canada may follow from the fact that 92 percent of Americans in this category, but only 62 percent of Canadians, are of at least the third generation. For women of Italian and Polish ances-

---

8 The study was restricted to non-official-language groups.

Table 5:   *Rates of Endogamy[a] among Native-Born Members of Selected Ethnic Groups and Sizes of Groups as Percentages of Total Population, Canada and United States*

| Ethnic Category | Canada | | | United States | |
| | Endogamy | | Percentage of 1981 Population | Endogamy 1980 | Percentage of 1980 Population |
	1971	1981			
British	50.0	74.2	40.2	—	44.0
English	65.6	—	—	56.1	21.9
Irish	26.9	—	—	39.5	17.7
Scottish	27.5	—	—	21.2	4.4
French	86.5	86.7	26.7	21.4	5.7
German	38.3	35.0	4.7	48.6	21.7
Italian	30.1	25.8	3.1	39.5	5.4
Dutch	65.2	26.3	1.7	19.3	2.8
Polish	24.1	13.6	1.1	29.8	3.6
Swedish	—	—	—	13.2	1.9
Norwegian	13.6	13.2	1.2	22.0	1.5
Danish	—	—	—	9.0	0.7
Ukrainian	45.0	36.0	2.2	—	—

[a] Female endogamy, except for 1971 in Canada.

Sources: Richard 1991, 110 (Canada); Richard forthcoming, table 8.3 (Canada); Lieberson and Waters 1988, 34, 173 (United States).

try, the rates of endogamy are considerably higher in the United States than they are in Canada. This is somewhat puzzling, given that these groups account for only a slightly larger proportion of total population in the United States and especially given that, in both groups, the percentage of people who belong to at least the third generation is much higher in the United States. Finally, the rate of endogamy is somewhat higher in Canada for women of Dutch ancestry but somewhat lower in Canada for women of Scandinavian ancestry. In both instances, the difference is relatively small. Given the generational composition of these groups in the two countries, however, one would have expected a much higher rate in Canada for both groups.

In short, these data for a limited number of groups do not indicate that the rate of assimilation is greater in the United States than it is in Canada. To the contrary, when the generational composition of groups is taken into account, it suggests that the "blending" of groups is proceeding at a faster rate in Canada, at least among some groups of European origin.

Multiple Origins

The children of interethnic marriages have a mixed cultural background. One can hypothesize that, as a result, their ethnic identity will be less crystallized and less salient than other dimensions of their selves. Of course, this outcome is not automatic; the hypothesis refers to a tendency. As interethnic marriages increase, so does the proportion of the population with mixed ancestries — a phenomenon that, over time, may blur ethnic boundaries (Krotki and Odynak 1990, 416).

In Canada, the proportion of census respondents that reported multiple origin was 27.6 percent in 1986 (Krotki and Odynak 1990, 433) and 28.9 percent in 1991 (Statistics Canada 1993). Multiple ancestry is more common in the United States: in the 1979 Current Population Survey (216,613 respondents), 46 percent of those who reported at least one specific ancestry reported at least one additional ancestry as well. In the 1980 census, the proportion was 37 percent (Lieberson and Waters 1988, 46). For most ethnic groups, the percentage of those with mixed ancestry is substantially higher or lower in one country than it is in the other.[9] For ten groups, the percentage is higher in the United States;[10] for six groups, it is higher in Canada;[11]

9 For Canada, the percentages are calculated from the 1986 census data in Table 1 in Krotki and Odynak (1990, 419). The data for the United States are the 1980 census data in Lieberson and Waters (1988, 45). In the calculation of percentages, persons with multiple ancestries are counted as such in each of the ethnic categories involved. For example, a person of Polish and English ancestries is counted as both multiple-origin Polish and multiple-origin English.

10 English, French, Scottish, Italian, Dutch, Portuguese, Hungarian, Greek, Danish, and Swiss.

11 Irish, Polish, Norwegian, Swedish, Russian, and Romanian.

and for two it is about the same.[12] In view of the difference in the generational composition of the various ethnic groups in Canada and the United States, it is surprising that the number of groups for which the percentage of members with multiple origins is higher in Canada is as large as it is. The blending of groups can only take place over generations; consequently, if blending were occurring at the same rate in the two countries, it would be more advanced in the United States. The above results suggest that it is occurring more rapidly in Canada, at least for some groups.

Linguistic Retention

The extent of knowledge, use, and transmission to the next generation of the group language is another measure of cultural retention. Language is a vital component of culture, although it is not equally so for all groups. For some, its loss seems to be close to complete acculturation; others can abandon it and yet retain other cultural elements.

How do ethnic minorities in Canada and in the United States compare according to this measure of cultural retention? In 1982, 89 percent of the US population five years of age and over spoke only English at home. In Canada, it is estimated that in 1986 between 88 and 90 percent spoke one of the two official languages at home (Lachapelle and Grenier 1988, 22–23).

A large-scale US survey (150,000 respondents) carried out in 1976 found that 9 percent of adults whose first language was not English spoke only the minority language and 14.9 percent spoke some English as well; the other 76.1 percent spoke mostly or only English (Stevens 1992, 178). There are, of course, important differences in this regard among minority groups and between native-born and foreign-born respondents.

Table 6 shows the percentages of foreign-born and native-born members of several minority language groups in Canada and in the

---

12 German and Welsh.

Table 6: *Usual Use of a Language Other Than English by Selected Ethnic Group, Canada and the United States, 1976*

(persons aged 14 and over)

Language Group	Native-Born		Foreign-Born	
	Canada	United States	Canada	United States
		(percentage)		
Chinese	39.6	10.0	79.4	65.9
Dutch	4.2	—	18.9	—
German	6.1	3.6	34.6	7.7
Greek	52.5	2.5	80.4	53.4
Hungarian	8.4	—	50.7	—
Italian	29.2	1.4	73.9	34.8
Japanese	—	9.7	—	46.6
Polish	8.0	2.3	55.1	35.2
Portuguese	56.9	3.5	79.5	62.1
Russian	—	1.0	—	12.3
Scandinavian	1.0	0.4	12.7	5.1
Spanish groups	—	35.2	—	71.0
Ukrainian	11.3	—	65.0	—

Sources: Statistics Canada, special tabulation (Canada); Veltman 1983, 49, 59 (United States).

United States who use the ethnic language. The table suggests several observations. First, the incidence of ethnic-language use appears to be higher in Canada, among both native-born and foreign-born persons, than it is in the United States. It should be noted, however, that the data for Canada refer to the language most often spoken at home, whereas the data for the United States (Veltman 1983, 48–59) refer to the language usually spoken. Since the interviews for the US survey were conducted in the home, the respondents may have tended to answer in relation to that setting. However, it is possible that they had other settings in mind — the workplace, for example. To the extent that this is the case, as Veltman notes (1983, 32–33), the survey may have overestimated the extent of language loss. Certainly the Canadian percentages would have been lower had the respondents been asked about their use of the ethnic language throughout the day, rather than about its use in the home only. It is likely, therefore, that this comparison overstates the difference between the two countries.[13]

A second observation is that the proportion of people who usually use a language other than English varies significantly from group to group. Among the foreign-born, it varies from 12.7 to 80.4 percent in Canada and from 5.1 to 71.0 percent in the United States. Among the native born, the variation is less pronounced: the proportions range from 1 to 56.7 percent in Canada and from 0.4 to 35.2 percent in the United States.[14] The acculturation process has a leveling effect across the various language groups.

Third, in both countries, the native-born are much less likely than the foreign-born to use the ethnic language. A further analysis of the US data shows that the nativity of the parents significantly affects the probability that their children will use a language other than English; if both parents are foreign-born, 72.8 percent of the children speak a language other than English; the figure is 18.7 percent if one parent is native-born and 15.6 percent if both parents are native-born (Stevens 1985, 79).[15]

Other studies show similar patterns of language loss in both countries. In the Albany survey, 10.9 percent of native-born whites could speak their mother tongue and 4.6 percent used it in their daily lives (Alba 1990, 95–98). Since there were very few individuals of Spanish origin in the Albany sample (Alba 1990, 33), the figure for foreign language use among native-born whites fits well with the

---

13 Canadians in the English-speaking provinces may be closer to Americans than Canadians in Quebec are in their degree of ethnic-language retention. The 1986 census data show that, in several ethnic groups, the percentage of people who reported the ethnic language as their mother tongue was lower in English Canada than it was in Quebec (Kralt and Pendakur 1991, 8–9).

14 In both countries, and for both native-born and foreign-born, the incidence is lowest among people of Scandinavian descent.

15 The Stevens results, like those reported by Veltman (1983), are based on the 1976 Survey of Income and Education.

figure (5.7 percent) obtained for the non-Spanish groups in the 1976 national survey noted above.

In Canada, the 1973 Non-Official Language Study showed that knowledge and use of the ethnic language decreases markedly over generations. Although 71 percent of the first-generation respondents were fluent in their ethnic language, no fourth-generation respondents were fluent; the percentage with no knowledge at all increased from 1.9 to 81.2. The results for language use were almost identical (O'Bryan, Reitz, and Kuplowska 1976, 45–46, 53–55).[16]

The same survey also addressed fluency in the group language, by generation, for selected ethnic groups (O'Bryan, Reitz, and Kuplowska 1976, 45–46). The results show the same patterns as the US data presented earlier. First, the proportion of respondents who are fluent in the ethnic language varies considerably from group to group, from 22.6 percent among respondents of Scandinavian origin to 78.8 percent among those of Greek origin. Second, the variations are less pronounced in the second and third generations than they are in the first. Third, the decline in the knowledge of the group language from the first to the third generation is very sizable: 70.8 percent declare a fluency in the language in the first generation; only 0.6 percent do so in the third and subsequent generations.

Reitz (1980b, 114, 131) constructed an index of language retention that used several indicators: language knowledge, language use, listening to ethnic radio, and reading the ethnic-language press. Although 78.9 percent of adult immigrants and 55.8 percent of childhood immigrants had high scores on this index, the figures for second- and third-generation respondents were only 16.2 percent and 3.2 percent, respectively.

---

16 The process of language shift begins in the immigrant generation. In the United States, Veltman (1983) found, the percentage of immigrants who use a language other than English diminishes progressively as the length of stay in the country increases: among non-Spanish language groups, the use of a language other than English was 56.5 percent among immigrants who had arrived in the 1970s, 39.6 percent among immigrants who had arrived during the 1960s, and 19.9 percent among immigrants who had arrived before the 1960s. The corresponding percentages for Spanish-speaking immigrants were 87.8, 70.1, and 58.1.

Social Interaction
and Social Activities

Cultural maintenance or loss should manifest itself in the composition of social networks. Depending on the salience of the culture, there should be more or less overlap between one's ethnic origin and the origin of one's friends. If ethnicity does not matter, the proportion of persons of the same ethnic origin in a friendship network should not differ significantly from the proportion that would occur on a random basis, given the proportion of individuals of that origin in the population.

In the 1973 Non-Official Language Study, "about one third of the sample is completely embedded in the ethnic group social networks, another third is completely outside such networks and the final third straddles the first two groups" (Reitz 1980b, 112). An index of informal interaction within ethnic groups showed a strong relationship between the degree of interaction and generation: 72.4 percent of adult immigrants but only 20.8 percent of third-generation respondents scored high on the index.[17] The 1979 Toronto study obtained similar results (Isajiw 1990, 57).

The pattern of involvement in organized activities is the same. According to the 1973 Non-Official Languages Study, ethnic church affiliation declined from 57.3 percent among adult immigrants to 51.3 percent among childhood immigrants, to 24.1 percent among second-generation respondents, and to 13 percent among third-generation respondents (Reitz 1980b, 131). The 1979 Toronto study found that participation in ethnic functions also declined across generations, although, as in the case of friendships, the decline did not take place at the same rate in all groups (Isajiw 1990, 62).[18]

The Albany study obtained similar results: "[a]pproximately a third of the top five friendships of native-born whites involve some

---

17 The index included three indicators: the maintenance of close ties within the respondent's group, the ethnicity of the people that the respondent visits in their homes, and the ethnic composition of the respondent's friendship ties.

18 The functions included picnics, concerts, rallies, dances, parties, and public lectures. The results were for German, Italian, Jewish, and Ukrainian respondents.

degree of ethnic overlap,...a figure that in all probability is greater than it would be if friendships were formed without regard to ethnicity" (Alba 1990, 213). In 41.7 percent of the sample, there was no overlap at all, and 24.6 percent did not know the ethnic ancestry of their friends (Alba 1990, 213). The study also found that 1.1 percent of native-born white members of voluntary associations belonged to one that was "ethnic, racial, or nationality" (Alba 1990, 241) and 27.2 percent attended or participated in ethnic festivals or celebrations (Alba 1990, 79). The second percentage is somewhat lower than those found for second- and third-generation persons in four different ethnic groups in Toronto (Isajiw 1990, 62). The difference may be attributable to the differences in the composition of the two samples or to the fact that, in the Toronto study, "group functions" included a wider range of activities.

These results do not show a striking difference between the two countries. If anything, the importance of ethnicity in social networks and social participation may be greater in the United States, if one considers that most ethnic groups in the United States are "older" than their counterparts in Canada. Indeed, in the Albany study, the proportion of members of at least third-generation standing is less than 70 percent in only one of the nine ethnic groups surveyed; it is less than 80 percent in only two of the groups (Alba 1990, 33).

Summary

In this chapter, we have attempted to ascertain whether ethnic minorities are in fact more likely to retain their identity and culture in Canada than in the United States. We have considered data related to five aspects of the question: (1) the salience of ethnicity, as measured in terms of individuals' knowledge of their ancestry, the extent to which individuals identify with a particular ethnic group, and the importance they attach to their ancestry; (2) intermarriage; (3) multiple origins; (4) linguistic retention; and (5) social interaction and activities.

Although it is not possible to draw a firm conclusion from the available evidence, uncertainty about personal ancestry seems to be somewhat more common in the United States than it is in Canada.

This is so, perhaps primarily because the proportion of third- and fourth-generation individuals in ethnic groups of European origin is much higher in the United States than it is in Canada. As the generations accumulate, knowledge of ancestry declines — in great part because of intermarriages and the resulting multiple ancestries.

The level of ethnic identification appears to be much the same in the two countries. In both countries, the proportions of those who identify themselves as members of an ethnic group, as "Canadian" or "American," or as "hyphenated" varies considerably from survey to survey. This variation may reflect variation in the wording or the timing of the survey or in the characteristics of the sample. In general, however, there is no clear indication that ethnic origin has more salience for Canadians than it does for Americans.

The data on intermarriage and multiple origins do not suggest that the United States is more assimilationist than Canada. Intermarriage is fairly common in both countries, and it increases from generation to generation at about the same rate in both of them. There are, of course, important variations among ethnic groups: in general, large groups show a higher incidence of marriage within the group than do small groups. The rates of endogamy for each generation vary from group to group as well.

Although the incidence of ethnic language loss is high in both countries, the overall results suggest that it is higher in the United States. The difference may be attributable, however, to the nature of the available data: the Canadian data refer to the language used in the home, whereas the American data refer to the language "usually" spoken. In addition, the generational data available indicate the same pattern in both countries of language loss over time: by the third generation, knowledge and use of the ethnic language is very low in both countries.

Finally, we found little difference between the two countries in the importance of ethnicity to the formation of social ties or to patterns of social participation.

As we have noted throughout the discussion, the available evidence did not allow us to make conclusive comparisons. Indeed, a number of hypotheses about the phenomenon of cultural maintenance could not be examined at all. It is possible, for instance, that, although some elements of ethnic cultures are abandoned, others persist in new forms, changing as circumstances change (Yancey, Eriksen, and Juliani 1976). Also, although ethnic cultures may have ever less effect on the ways in which people organize their social relations and activities, they may remain present to a degree in the culture at large. Again, although ethnic culture may matter less and less to most members of ethnic collectivities, it may become more important among professionals and intellectuals connected with academic, artistic, literary, and other cultural institutions. Such changes in the manifestation of ethnic identity and culture may follow different patterns in the two countries. Any such differences might be the result of differences in social context, differences in government policy, or both.

Generally, however, Gans' (1979) analysis of the contemporary relevance of ethnicity in US society appears to apply to both countries. Gans' view is that, by the third generation, ethnicity has become symbolic; that is to say, "people are less and less interested in their ethnic cultures and organizations — both sacred and secular — and are instead more concerned with maintaining their identity" (Gans 1979, 77). That is, although people tend to retain their ethnic identities, these identities do not shape their behavior or their social relationships. Gans' review of research confirmed the conclusion that Kralt drew from his analysis of 1971 census data — namely, "that Canadian society is not the multi-cultural society it is often considered to be" (Kralt 1977, 81). Members of ethnic groups, generally, "become part of the wider Canadian industrial society with minimal importance attached to ethnic origin" (Kralt 1977, 82).

We noted earlier that groups of European origin in the United States are primarily third generation or older, while in Canada they consist mainly of first- and second-generation persons. Given this difference in generational composition, Gans' hypothesis would have more application to the United States than to Canada (Weinfeld 1981). Nevertheless, the research results that we have considered in this chapter suggest that both countries are moving toward "symbolic ethnicity" at about the same pace — a movement, it should be recalled, that can be observed clearly only over generations.

Chapter 4

Prejudice and Discrimination

How do Canadians and Americans compare in terms of racial and ethnic prejudice and discrimination? In this chapter, we shall attempt to answer this question, using not only measures of overt prejudice but also measures of the extent to which people in the two countries uphold negative stereotypes of minorities, seek to maintain "social distance" between themselves and members of other groups (in this context, our analysis will consider attitudes toward immigration, minorities as neighbors, and intermarriage), and withhold support from government's taking action against discrimination. We shall also examine evidence, derived from "field trials," of direct discrimination in employment.

Prejudice is a matter of attitudes, discrimination is a matter of behavior. Both things are difficult to measure. Racial and ethnic prejudice has become much less socially acceptable than it once was. Discrimination in employment or housing is not only less socially acceptable, it is illegal. Many observers argue, however, that prejudice and discrimination persist in concealed form. People hide their real attitudes, discriminate in a covert manner, and tolerate discriminatory institutions. It is not easy to turn these attitudes and this behavior out into the daylight, as writers from Gordon Allport (1954) to Studs Terkel (1992) have found.

Our purpose here is not to resolve the problems of measurement. Rather, it is to see whether the standard indicators of prejudice and discrimination, which are perhaps flawed, suggest in any way that there is a difference between the level of prejudice and discrimination in Canada and the level in the United States. The familiar Canadian assumption that the level in Canada is lower can, we believe, be meaningfully addressed in this way.

Trends within Each Country

In both Canada and the United States, a range of indicators of racial attitudes show certain positive trends. The National Academy of Sciences report, *A Common Destiny: Blacks and American Society* (Jaynes and Williams 1989), gleaned data from dozens of national opinion polls conducted between 1942 and 1983. These polls, the results of which are summarized in Table 7, show growing and now virtually universal verbal commitment to the principle of racial equality. White preferences for "social distance" from blacks in various settings have declined significantly. Although popular support for government policies and programs to assist blacks remains low and has shown no consistent trend over time, there has been no major white "backlash."

In Canada, race is less salient, and there is less research.[1] Without doubt the climate in Canada too has improved since the Second World War, when racially exclusionary immigration policies were still in effect. For its study, *The Economic and Social Impact of Immigration*, the Economic Council of Canada assembled data from existing surveys of intolerance (Swan 1991, 111–113). The council reported a "positive" trend among anglophones on an index of "tolerance." However, the study did not present specific quantitative results, and the index included items on gender as well as race. Henry's finding that one Torontonian in six expresses "very racist" views (Henry 1978, 1) is similarly difficult to compare with other studies, since the index of racism is a combination of 29 correlated items that address a complex range of perceptions and attitudes.

---

1 For a review of the Canadian research, see Henry 1986.

Table 7: Trends in Racial Attitudes among Whites in the United States

Type of Question	Question	First and Last Year Asked	Percent Change from First to Last Year	Percent Positive Last Time Asked
Principle	Same schools	1942/1982	+ 58	90
	Equal jobs	1944/1972	+ 52	97
	Same transportation	1942/1970	+ 42	88
	Residential choice (NORC)[a]	1963/1982	+ 32	71
	Residential choice (ISR)	1964/1976	+ 23	88
	Same accommodations	1963/1970	+ 15	88
	Black candidate (Gallup)	1958/1983	+ 44	81
	Black candidate (NORC)	1972/1983	+ 12	85
	Against intermarriage laws	1963/1982	+ 28	66
	Intermarriage	1958/1983	+ 36	40
	General segregation[b]	1964/1978	+ 8	35
Implementation	Federal job intervention	1964/1974	− 2	36
	Open housing	1973/1983	+ 12	46
	Federal school intervention	1964/1978	− 17	25
	Busing (ISR)	1972/1980	0	9
	Busing (NORC)	1972/1983	+ 6	21
	Accommodations intervention	1964/1974	+ 22	66
	Spending on blacks	1973/1983	− 1	26
	Aid to minorities	1970/1982	− 4	18
Social distance	Few (Gallup)	1958/1980	+ 20	95
	Few (NORC)	1972/1983	+ 2	95
	Half (Gallup)	1958/1980	+ 26	76
	Half (NORC)	1972/1983	0	76
	Most (Gallup)	1958/1980	+ 9	42
	Most (NORC)	1972/1983	− 6	37
	Next door	1958/1978	+ 30	86
	Great numbers	1958/1978	+ 26	46
	Same block	1942/1972	+ 49	85
	Black dinner guest	1963/1982	+ 26	78
Miscellaneous	Thermometer rating[c] of blacks	1964/1982	+ 1	61
	Ku Klux Klan rating[d]	1965/1979	− 13	71
	Intelligence	1942/1968	+ 30	77
	Civil rights push	1964/1980	+ 6	9
	Black push	1963/1982	+ 18	39

Note: NORC is the National Opinion Research Center; ISR is the Institute for Social Research.

[a] This item uses a Likert scale response format. The percentages reported involve a combination of "disagree slightly" and "disagree strongly" responses.

[b] The trend for this item is probably affected by a contextual linkage to the federal school intervention implementation item.

[c] The feeling thermometer is a standard question used in the National Election Study. It calls for respondents to rank groups or individuals on a 100 point scale, where 0 indicates very cold feelings, 50 indicates neutral feelings, and 100 indicates very warm feelings.

[d] The rating scale runs from − 5 to + 5. The figures reported indicate the percentage of people giving "highly unfavorable" ratings of the Ku Klux Klan (scores of − 4 or − 5).

Source: The table is from Jaynes and Williams 1989, 122–123. It is based on data from Schoman et al. 1985; and Bobo 1987.

These parallel attempts at trend analysis invite several observations. First, data on racial attitudes in Canada are so much less plentiful than data on attitudes in the United States that clear comparisons are difficult. Second, the existence of positive trends in racial attitudes in both countries may be a point of similarity between them, even if in some ways these changes prove superficial. Definitive comparison must focus on specific key areas, an approach that, as we shall show, yields interesting results. And third, the comparative data are very time-sensitive. One cannot meaningfully compare US data from the 1960s with Canadian data from the 1970s or 1980s. In fact, our goal here is really to measure the trajectory of change in the two countries. One might say that what is at issue is not the extent of cross-national differences, but the approximate number of years (if any) that one country may be ahead of the other in terms of changes in racial attitudes.

Overt Racism and Negative Racial Stereotypes

US survey research clearly shows that overt racism, by which we mean the explicit assertion of innate white superiority, is now expressed only by a small minority. Schuman, Steeh, and Bobo (1985, 125) show that, as recently as the 1940s, only 50 to 60 percent of Americans outside the South — and even fewer in the South — endorsed the innate equality of blacks, agreeing that "Negroes are as intelligent as white people" and can "learn things just as well if they are given the same education and training." Since the 1950s, the proportion has been at least 90 percent.[2]

A survey conducted in 1990 by Decima Research Ltd. permits a comparison of the two countries. The Canadians in the survey were, overall, slightly less overtly racist than the Americans, but only slightly: 90 percent of the Canadians, and 86 percent of the Ameri-

---

2 According to a poll conducted in 1989 by the *Los Angeles Times*, 90 per cent of the population of Los Angeles said that "blacks are as intelligent as white people — that is, blacks learn just as well if they are given the same education." The percentage among "WASPs" was 92 percent.

cans agreed that "all races are created equal" (*Maclean's* 1990). This difference is insubstantial. Large majorities in both countries deny overt racism.

The denial of overt racism in both countries is also reflected in the fact that few people support organizations with explicitly racist philosophies. The 1989 National Academy of Sciences study (Jaynes and Williams 1989) found that, in the United States, support for the Ku Klux Klan had increased somewhat during the late 1960s and 1970s but was still marginal. KKK groups in Canada and indigenous organizations with racist messages, such as the Western Guard or the Heritage Front, also have few members (Barrett 1987; Sher 1983; and see Schoenfeld 1991). Actually, many supporters of groups such as the KKK deny that they are racists. One-third of the respondents in a survey conducted in and near Chattanooga, Tennessee, had favorable views of the KKK. Many of them cited the KKK as a "charitable" organization and as one that supported law and order; they may have been dissembling their knowledge of its racial views (Seltzer and Lopes 1986, 95). In both countries, some mainstream politicians, too, have been accused of appealing to hidden racial feelings, though as a rule they deny this intention.

How widespread are hidden racist attitudes? Is there more hidden racism in one country than the other? When racism is discussed in public debate, the reference is often really not to overt racism but rather to hidden racism, or to negative racial stereotyping. To what extent do people hold views that might reflect an unexpressed belief in white superiority?

US attitude surveys show that some of those who deny racism in fact have racist views that are easily brought to the surface. For example, when Americans are asked to explain why so many blacks are poor, many of them refer to innate racial inferiority. The General Social Surveys (GSS) for 1988 and 1989 asked the following question:

> On the average blacks have worse jobs, income, and housing than white people. Do you think that these differences are...(a) mainly due to discrimination, (b) because most blacks have less in-born ability to learn, (c) because most blacks don't have the chance for education that it takes to rise out of poverty, and

(d) because most blacks just don't have the motivation or will power to pull themselves out of poverty? (Kluegel 1990, 514.)

The proportion of respondents who chose the explanation "blacks have less in-born ability," either alone or in combination with other explanations, was 20.8 percent (Kluegel 1990, 517). Thus, although few whites explicitly challenge the proposition (put forward in the 1990 Decima survey, for example) that all races are created equal, a significantly larger proportion refer to inherent racial inferiority when asked to explain black poverty. Some people explain black disadvantage as "God's plan" (Kluegel and Smith 1986, 188).

Many Americans, in shifting away from overt racist views, have embraced what Kluegel calls "individualistic" explanations for black-white inequality (Kluegel 1990, 515). They say that blacks lack motivation or have an inferior culture. They deny "structuralist" explanations — that blacks lack educational and employment opportunity or experience discrimination. In the 1977 GSS, the proportion of respondents who explained black poverty by reference to innate black inferiority was 26 percent (Kluegel and Smith 1986, 188; see also Sniderman and Hagen 1985, 30). In 1988–89, as we have shown, it was about 21 percent. Throughout this period, most endorsed individualist explanations, and only about 25 to 30 percent believed that blacks experienced any significant discrimination. In fact, the 1977 GSS showed that the same proportion felt that blacks were given preference — that there was discrimination against whites (Kluegel 1985, 768). "Young and old Americans alike appear to believe that discrimination in the work force *currently* does not function to limit opportunity for black workers to any substantial degree" (Kluegel 1985, 771).

Does the belief that blacks bring disadvantage on themselves reflect racial prejudice? In many cases perhaps not, but Kluegel (1990, 516) shows that the two things are related empirically. In the United States, overt racists — those who say that blacks are disadvantaged because they are inferior — are the group most likely to believe that whites have the right to whites-only neighborhoods and to favor laws against intermarriage. Kluegel calls these matters "traditional indicators of prejudice," since they reflect a desire to exclude people on the basis of race.[3] However, although those who say that blacks bring disadvantage on themselves are less likely than the overt racists to have these traditional prejudices, they are more likely to have them than are those who cite discrimination to explain why blacks are disadvantaged. So those who cite black motivation are more likely than are those who cite discrimination to believe that black exclusion is justified.

What are the comparable Canadian attitudes? Canadian explanations for minority-group disadvantage are not, of course, strictly comparable with American explanations. Asking Canadians about minorities in Canada is obviously not necessarily the same as asking Americans about minorities in the United States. Nevertheless, in the 1987 Canadian Charter Study about 70 percent of the respondents agreed that "immigrants often bring discrimination upon themselves by their own personal attitudes and habits," 25 percent disagreed, and the remaining 5 percent gave various qualified responses or "don't know" (Sniderman et al. 1991).[4] The proportion of those who cited an "individualistic" explanation — 70 percent — is about the same as the proportion in the United States. Thus, Canadians, like Americans, frequently deny that the minorities in their respective countries are the victims of racial discrimination. Of course, it is arguable what is in fact the case in each country. We examine data relevant to the actual comparative extent of discrimination below. For now, we simply note that Canadians and Americans seem to be alike in tending to prefer individualistic explanations of minority disadvantage to explanations that cite discrimination.

Some interesting comparative data are available on racial jokes. In the 1990 Decima survey, more Americans than Canadians — 46 percent versus 38 percent — said they never told racial jokes.[5]

---

3 See our discussion of "social distance" below.

4 We would like to thank Joseph Fletcher for providing us with access to this information about the Charter Study.

5 *Maclean's*, June 25, 1990, 52. The proportions of Americans who rarely, sometimes, or often told ethnic or racial jokes were 25, 25, and 4 percent, respectively; the corresponding figures for Canadians were 28, 26, and 7 percent.

Americans may be more on guard against giving racial offense than Canadians are, perhaps because of the greater salience of racial conflict in the United States.

Anti-Semitism

In both countries, the Jewish group is long-established and largely urban, accounts for 1 to 2 percent of the population, and has high average levels of educational and occupational attainment and earnings (Lieberson and Waters 1988; Li 1988; Reitz 1990). Because of this similarity, comparisons of negative attitudes and behavior toward Jews provide a particularly good indication of relative predisposition toward ethnic tolerance. For Jews, unlike blacks, the issue of relations with the other groups arises in a very similar way in the two countries.

Studies that measure the prevalence of negative stereotypes of Jews have produced remarkably similar aggregate results in the United States and Canada. We compare results from the Charter Study in Canada in 1987 (Sniderman et al. 1992; 1993) with those from a US survey reported by Martire and Clark (1982, 17) in 1981. In three of the four comparisons, as Table 8 shows, about one Canadian in five and one American in five gave a response that described the Jewish group in a negative way. Canadians were more likely than Americans, however, to agree that Jews are "pushy."

There are positive stereotypes of the Jewish group as well as negative ones. Smith (1990, 9), using GSS data, found that, in the United States, the general population rates Jews above "whites" in relation to the descriptive tags "rich," "hard-working," "not violent," "intelligent," and "self-supporting."

In both countries, anti-Semitic stereotypes have their greatest currency within certain other minority groups. The frictions between Jews and these other minorities are secondary ethnic conflicts, derived from broader patterns of ethnic disadvantage. In Canada, French-Canadian attitudes toward Jews are more negative than those of any other group (Sniderman et al. 1991). However, French-

Table 8:   *Attitudes toward Jews in Canada and the United States*

United States (1981)		Canada (1987)	
1. "Jews don't care what happens to anyone but their own kind."		"Most Jews don't care what happens to people who aren't Jewish."	
Probably true:	16%	Agree:	19%
Probably false:	59%	Disagree:	68%
Not sure:	25%	Don't know:	12%
2. "Jews today are trying to push in where they are not wanted."		"Most Jews are pushy."	
Probably true:	16	Agree	34
Probably false:	70	Disagree	55
Not sure:	14	Don't know:	11
3. "Jews have contributed much to the cultural life of America."		"Jews have made an important contribution to the cultural life of Canada."	
Probably false:	14	Disagree:	21
Probably true:	53	Agree:	63
Not sure:	33	Don't know:	15
4. "Jews are more willing to use shady practices."		"Jews are more willing than others to use shady practices to get ahead."	
Probably true:	23	Agree:	23
Probably false:	46	Disagree:	61
Not sure:	31	Don't know:	14

Sources: The Canadian data are from the Charter Study (see Sniderman et al. 1991). Data were collected by the York University Institute of Behavioural Research in 1987 (2,080 in sample); the questions used here are numbers i15–i19. We thank Joseph Fletcher for providing access to these data. The US data were collected by Yankelovich, Skelly and White, Inc. in 1981 (1,072 in sample) and reported by Martire and Clark 1982, 17.

Canadian attitudes toward other minorities are also more negative. At the same time, there is greater pressure toward conformity — including ethnic assimilation — in Quebec than there is in the rest of the country. These are classic patterns in group conflict: suspicion of outsiders and closing of ranks among insiders.

In the United States, there is a roughly parallel tension between Jews and blacks. This tension is at least in part the result of a reactive response among blacks, rather than an indication that blacks have a greater predisposition to anti-Semitism than other groups. The position of blacks in the United States has also lead to tensions between blacks and other minorities, including Asians and Hispanics (Oliver and Johnson 1984; Johnson and Oliver 1989; Rose 1989).

One can compare anti-Semitic behavior in the United States and Canada by using the "audit of anti-Semitic incidents" that B'nai Brith, the Jewish service organization, publishes in each country. The Anti-Defamation League of B'nai Brith in the United States reports 1,879 incidents in 1991 (ADLBB 1991, 29). In Canada, the equivalent organization is the League for Human Rights of B'nai Brith, whose more positive-sounding name suggests a less conflictful or more tolerant setting. Nevertheless, the number of incidents reported in Canada in 1991 was 251 (LHRBB Canada 1991, 4), more than might be expected given the roughly 10-to-1 US-Canadian population ratio. The totals for 1982 to 1992, however, uphold the ratio — there were 12,665 incidents in the United States and 1,191 in Canada. The year-to-year figures fluctuate not quite in lock step, responding similarly to events such as the Persian Gulf war, which seemed to provoke increases in anti-Semitic incidents — and anti-Muslim incidents as well — in both countries.[6]

Thus, attitudes and behavior reflect very similar patterns of anti-Semitism in the two countries. This case, free from some of the methodological complexities that affect other comparisons, does not support the hypothesis that Canadians are more tolerant than Americans.

Social Distance

Social distance is a measure of dominant-group tolerance for social relations with members of a given minority. For a given minority,

---

6 Incident classification indicates that vandalism is more prevalent in the US reports, harassment in the Canadian. Shefman (1987, 6) states that the difference "may, in part, be attributed to the different legal and social traditions in Canada which demand action against prejudice and bigotry prior to action being taken." However, this *ad hoc* explanation does not account for the higher rates of harassment in Canada. Perhaps the reporting criteria vary.

social distance is greater when the majority is unwilling to tolerate not only close relations such as marriage and family membership but also more distant relations. Thus, the majority may be unwilling to tolerate members of the minority as neighbors, as co-workers, or even as immigrants.

US data show that social distances from the dominant English-origin group are greatest for blacks and other racial minorities, less for southern Europeans, and least for northern Europeans (Bogardus 1958, 1967). Surveys of university social science students conducted since the 1920s have shown that social distance for a variety of minority groups has declined over the years but that the rank-order of racial groups has remained fairly stable (see Owen, Eisner, and McFaul 1981; and Sinha and Barry 1991). Table 9 shows how racial and ethnic groups in the United States have been ranked in various years. Sinha and Berry (1991), who have applied the concept of social distance to groups such as intravenous drug users, AIDS victims, people who have attempted suicide, and homosexuals, find that ethnic and racial groups are now less socially distant from the dominant groups than are these other groups. They suggest that race and ethnicity are becoming less important than behavior as a basis for discrimination.

Comparative Canadian data are available for national samples as well as student populations. The national data describe the "social standing" of ethnic and racial groups, which is presumably akin to social distance or group prestige. In a national survey on ethnic social standing, English- and French-Canadian respondents placed group names in ranked categories. The results in Table 10 show a rank-order similar to the rank-order for US minorities in Table 9. Racial minorities, including blacks and Asians, are at the bottom, southern Europeans rank higher, and northern Europeans higher still (Berry Kalin, and Taylor 1977; Pineo 1977, and Angus Reid Group Inc. 1991). Driedger and Mezoff (1981) derive similar results from data on Manitoba university students (see also Dion 1985).

Calculations of social distance index values on the basis of student samples yield similar results for the two countries. The 1977

Table 9: *Mean Social Distances of Ethnic and Racial Groups in the United States, 1926–90*

(as measured on the Bogardus social distance scale)

	1926	1946	1956	1966	1977	1990
Groups included in the Bogardus scale						
Americans (US white)	1.10	1.04	1.08	1.07	1.25	1.13
English	1.06	1.13	1.23	1.14	1.39	1.15
Canadians	1.13	1.11	1.16	1.15	1.42	1.19
Italians	1.94	2.28	1.89	1.51	1.65	1.36
French	1.32	1.31	1.47	1.36	1.58	1.37
Germans	1.46	1.59	1.61	1.54	1.87	1.39
American Indians	2.38	2.45	2.35	2.18	1.84	1.59
Poles	2.01	1.84	2.07	1.98	2.11	1.68
Jews	2.39	2.32	2.15	1.97	2.01	1.71
Blacks	3.28	3.60	2.74	2.56	2.03	1.73
Chinese	3.36	2.50	2.68	2.34	2.29	1.76
Japanese	2.80	3.61	2.70	2.41	2.38	1.86
Russians	1.88	1.83	2.56	2.38	2.57	1.93
Koreans	3.60	3.05	2.83	2.51	2.63	1.94
Mexicans	2.69	2.89	2.79	2.56	2.40	2.00
Groups not included in the Bogardus scale						
Israelis	—	—	—	—	—	2.63
Palestinians	—	—	—	—	—	2.78
Iranians	—	—	—	—	—	3.03
Spread	2.54	2.57	1.75	1.49	1.38	1.90
Change in spread		+ 0.03	− 0.82	− 0.26	− 0.11	+ 0.52

Note: The Bogardus social distance scale ranges from a low of 1.00 to a high of 7.00. The figures are based on mean ratings of the degree of distance that respondents would prefer to maintain between themselves and members of each group. The available responses are: acceptance "into my family through marriage or cohabitation" (1.00), acceptance "as close friends or room mate" (2.00), acceptance "in my dorm" (3.00), acceptance "as a co-worker or class mate" (4.00), acceptance "as speaking acquaintance only" (5.00), acceptance "as visitors only to my country" (6.00), and "would not accept into my country" (7.00).

Source: Sinha and Berry 1991, 7.

Table 10: *Social Standing of Minority Groups*
in English and French Canada

Minority Group	Social Standing as Ranked by:	
	English Canada	French Canada
Own group	83.1	77.6
English	82.4	77.6
Italians	43.1	51.3
French	60.1	72.4
Germans	48.7	40.5
Canadian Indians	28.3	32.5
Poles	42.0	38.0
Jews	46.1	43.1
Blacks	25.4	23.5
Chinese	33.1	24.9
Japanese	34.7	27.8
Russians	35.8	33.2

Note: The categories are placed in order of the comparable groups in Table 9; some groups
are not included.

Source: Pineo 1977, 154.

figure for blacks in the United States was 2.03 and a comparable
figure for blacks in Canada was 2.12; for West Indians it was 2.46
(Driedger and Mezoff 1981).7 For Chinese, the 1977 US figure was
2.29, and the 1981 Canadian figure was 2.33. For Mexicans, the US
and Canadian figures were, respectively, 2.40 and 2.38; for Japanese,
they were 2.38 and 2.40. There is one major discrepancy: the index
value for American Indians in 1977 was 1.84, whereas the value for
Native Indians in Canada, or at least in Manitoba, was substantially
higher, 2.70.

No one has calculated precise index values for social distance
between whites and specific minorities in both countries on the basis

---

7   A 1976 Toronto survey of the general population showed an index for blacks of
1.95. For East Indians, the index was 2.04; for Pakistanis, 2.22; and for Italians,
1.34. (Henry 1978, 83).

of national or even general-population data, let alone data collected at comparable points in time. As Table 7 has shown, Jaynes and Williams (1989, 122–123) summarized US national survey data to demonstrate that white social distances from blacks have declined. These and other potentially comparable data address specific components of social distance, such as acceptance of minorities as neighbors, or as family members through intermarriage, rather than social distance generally. The following subsections consider four of these specific components.

Immigration

One component of social distance is attitudes toward specific groups as immigrants. Canadians favor immigration more than Americans do, despite the fact that racial-minority immigration is currently greater in Canada. In the 1990 Decima survey, 58 percent of Americans wanted less immigration and only 6 percent wanted more (*Maclean's* 1990, 52). By contrast, 39 percent of Canadians wanted less immigration and 18 percent wanted more. Whether these more positive Canadian attitudes apply to "new" racial-minority immigrants is not clear. Nevertheless, in a 1976 Gallup poll, 63 percent of Canadians opposed racial restrictions and only 27 percent favored them. In 1981, only 10 percent supported "cutting off all non-white immigration to Canada."[8]

American attitudes toward immigration appear to have turned negative as immigration increased after the 1960s. In a series of comparable polls, the proportion of Americans who wanted less immigration increased from 33 percent in 1965 to 61 percent in 1993.[9] There appears to be a nearly comparable trend in Canada. Angus Reid Group Inc. (1989, 4–5) reports that the proportion of Canadians who think too many immigrants are coming to Canada increased

8 The Gallup Omnibus survey for the Minister of State for Multiculturalism in November 1981 showed 43 percent in complete agreement with "open immigration" and 56 percent at least partly in agreement.

9 *New York Times*, June 27, 1993, 1 and 16. The polls were conducted by Gallup and the *New York Times* in collaboration with CBS News.

from 30 percent in May 1988 to 31 percent in February 1989 and 43 percent in August 1989. An Ekos Research Associates Inc. poll showed that this proportion had risen to 53 percent by February 1994 (*Globe and Mail* [Toronto], March 10, 1994, p. A1). On the other hand, Environics polls conducted in 1986 and 1989 showed a decline in agreement with the statement that "there is too much immigration to Canada," from 66 percent to 57 percent (Angus Reid Group Ltd. 1989, 5).[10]

Canadians' somewhat more positive attitudes may reflect their country's different historical and institutional context, rather than cultural predisposition. Postwar Canadian immigration, mostly European in origin, has been a major element of economic and social development policy. Reimers and Troper (1992) argue that, in the United States, immigration has ceased to be a development policy and is now perceived as social welfare, and that public support has declined accordingly. Like Americans, and perhaps for similar reasons, Britons support racial minority immigration less than Canadians do. British immigration has been an obligation to former colonial territories in the Commonwealth, rather than a program of national development (see Reitz 1988a; 1988b).

At the same time, there are signs that growing unease with immigration among white Canadians as well as among white Americans is, in fact, related to race, not just to numbers or to immigration goals. In a 1979 survey in Toronto (Breton et al. 1990, 204), 63 percent of "majority Canadians" agreed that "present immigration laws make it too easy for certain groups to come to Canada." In identifying these "certain groups," respondents mentioned racial minorities three times more often than they mentioned other immigrant groups. European-origin immigrants shared these concerns. In the United States, a recent *Newsweek* poll asked a comparable question in a national sample: "Should it be easier or more difficult for people from the following places to immigrate to the US?" About half of the

---

10 The greater opposition to immigration in the Environics polls may result from a positive-response bias. The Angus Reid question allowed respondents to say whether the numbers of immigrants were too many, about right, or too few.

respondents said that it should be more difficult for people from China or other Asian countries to immigrate to the United States, and 61 percent said it should be more difficult for people from the Middle East to immigrate to the United States.[11] These results from the two countries seem to be roughly parallel.

Community and Neighborhood Residence

There has long been a significant cross-national difference in responses to racial minorities as neighbors. Comparative Gallup data assembled by Michalos (1982, 169, 206) indicate that in 1963 only 3 percent of Canadians said that they would definitely move "if colored people came to live next door" and 91 percent said that they would stay put. In the United States at that time, 20 percent said that they would move and only 55 percent said that they would stay.

Things have changed since the 1960s, of course. Although racial preferences for neighbors are still significant and strong in the United States, feelings have relaxed noticeably over time. In the late 1960s, US movers declined to 12 percent and stayers rose to 65 percent. In 1978, only 10 percent would move if a black moved next door (Schuman, Steeh, and Bobo 1985, 106–108). As late as 1981, however, a majority of northerners preferred a mostly white neighborhood and one in four preferred an all-white neighborhood (Schuman, Steeh, and Bobo 1985, 67). In the South, two-thirds preferred a mostly white neighborhood and the preference for an all-white neighborhood varied between 38 and 51 percent.[12] Openness to black neighbors varies with the numbers of blacks mentioned in the question. Figures in Table 7, above, show that, whereas only 46 percent of white Americans said they would not move if blacks came into their neighborhood in "great numbers," about 85 percent said they would not move if blacks moved in "next door" or onto the "same block."

---

11 *Newsweek*, August 9, 1993, 25.

12 The higher figure resulted from face-to-face interviews — in which, the authors suggest, the respondents could be sure that the interviewer was not black.

Canadian attitudes may not be markedly different, but in recent available surveys the same questions have not been asked. Replies to the most closely comparable questions do not suggest extreme cross-national differences. In the 1978–79 Ethnic Pluralism Survey in Toronto, two-thirds of the respondents said that they were willing to have a West Indian as a next-door neighbor "if you were completely free to decide yourself" (Breton et al. 1990, 200). The proportion that responded positively to having Chinese, Italian, or Portuguese neighbors was about 85 percent.

Acceptance into Social Clubs

A willingness to accept racial minorities into private clubs would seem to indicate an even greater tolerance than does a willingness to accept them into neighborhoods. Yet the data for both countries show more support for open membership than for open neighborhoods. In a 1987 Gallup poll, only 15 percent of Americans and 12 percent of Canadians though private clubs should have the right to exclude prospective members on the basis of race. The exclusion of minorities from social clubs may be regarded as a symbol of overt racism and may therefore be rejected even if there is a desire to exclude.

Intermarriage

Both Canadians and Americans have become more tolerant of racial intermarriage in recent decades, but Canadians continue to lead Americans in this regard. In Canada, disapproval of black-white marriages declined from 52 percent in 1968 to 35 percent in 1973 (Michalos 1982, 205), and those who disapprove are now only a small minority — 16 percent, according to a 1988 Gallup National Omnibus Newspaper poll. In 1988, according to the same poll, 72.5 percent of Canadians approved of black-white marriages. Lambert and Curtis (1984) show that English-Canadian disapproval declined from 60 percent in 1968 to 24 percent in 1983; there was less disapproval in Quebec.

In the United States, disapproval of black-white marriages declined from 72 percent in 1968 to 60 percent in 1972 (Michalos 1982, 205). Yet, in 1983, only 40 percent of Americans approved of marriages between whites and any non-whites (Schuman, Steeh, and Bobo 1985, 74–76). The 1988 GSS showed that 25 percent of Americans think black-white marriages should actually be outlawed (Niemi, Mueller, and Smith 1989, 170). This figure represents a decline from earlier decades, but clearly the social climate in the United States is different from the social climate in Canada. The 1989 Decima poll confirms the difference: 32 percent of the American respondents, but only 13 percent of the Canadians, said that they would be unhappy if one of their children "married someone from a different racial background." Only 15 percent of the Americans, but 25 percent of the Canadians, said that they would be "happy" (*Maclean's* 1989).

To put the differences in the context of change, attitudes in the United States today are like those in the Canada of a decade or more ago. The Canadian data cited above show a change of about 2 percentage points per year.[13] The US data in Jaynes and Williams (1989, 122) show a change of 1.5 points per year.[14] In the matter of opposition to intermarriage, two of the data sources cited above indicate a difference between the two countries of about 20 points.[15] Given a

---

13 This is based on a rough average from three sources: a decline of 37 points (from 53 to 16 percent opposed) in the Canada-wide data over the 20-year period 1968 through 1988 (1.85 points per year), a decline of 36 points (from 60 to 24 percent opposed) in the English-Canadian data over the 15-year period 1968 through 1983 (2.4 points per year), and a decline of 27 points (from 38 to 11 percent opposed) in the French-Canadian data over the same 15-year period (1.8 points per year).

14 The Jaynes and Williams data show a positive change of 36 points in attitudes toward intermarriage over a period of 25 years (1.4 points per year) and a positive change of 28 points in attitudes toward intermarriage laws over a period of 19 years (1.5 points per year).

15 The two sources are the 1968 Michalos data on black-white intermarriage (72 percent opposition in the United States, 52 percent in Canada) and the 1989 Decima data on unhappiness about interacial marriage by one's own children (32 percent in the United States, 13 percent in Canada).

rate of 1.5 or 2 points per year, therefore, Canada may be ten or a dozen years ahead of the United States in the trend toward acceptance of interracial marriages.

Employment Discrimination

How much ethnic or racial discrimination actually occurs in each of the two countries? We shift here from attitudes to behavior. Racial or ethnic discrimination in employment is defined as the commission of acts that put people at a disadvantage in the search for work or in the workplace solely because of their racial or ethnic origins. Our focus here is on discrimination against racial minorities. In both Canada and United States, as we shall show, most of the evidence suggests that discrimination against ethnic groups of European origin is not a major concern.

Discrimination is a complex phenomenon, and there are many different forms and sources of discrimination. Discrimination may be direct or indirect. Direct discrimination is a result of the unequal application of hiring criteria. It may be either overt or covert and, since overt discrimination is illegal, the research challenge is to identify covert discrimination. It may be either intentional or unintentional — a distinction of declining legal significance. And it may be motivated by any one or more of the following: negative attitudes toward racial minorities and a desire to exclude them, which human-capital economists call a "taste" for discrimination; negative stereotypes about the work potential of racial minorities, which are discriminatory when they are applied to an individual (whether or not the employer believes they are accurate for the group as a whole); economic incentives, which are a major topic of debate in economic and sociological discussions of labor markets; and social conventions or group pressures, such as when employee groups prefer, or are perceived to prefer, not to work with minorities.

Discrimination may also be indirect; that is, it may arise not from the unequal application of hiring criteria but from the discriminatory nature of the hiring criteria themselves. For example, discrimination may result indirectly from the established practice of "credentialism," or the use in hiring of educational criteria that are not actually related to the requirements of the job.[16]

One way to measure employment discrimination is to consider whether the occupations or earnings of racial minorities are commensurate with their job qualifications. We shall take up this question in Chapter 5, which examines the overall social and economic incorporation of minorities. Although there are risks in drawing conclusions about discrimination from analyses of this kind, we shall argue that a comparison of Canada and the United States on this basis is nonetheless relevant to an assessment of discrimination in the two countries.

Complaints of discrimination to human rights commissions offer another potential measure of employment discrimination, but such data almost certainly reflect only a very small proportion of all discriminatory acts. What is more important, the data are not comparable, since the procedures used by human rights commissions vary widely from one jurisdiction to another.

Here we shall consider findings from racial discrimination "field trials," which have been conducted in comparable ways in Canada and the United States. In these exercises, actors from different racial groups apply for the same jobs and present identical qualifications. Any differences in the employers' responses may reasonably be taken as evidence of direct discrimination.

In Toronto, field trials conducted in 1984 by Henry and Ginsberg (1985) found that whites received three times as many job offers as blacks. Blacks were five times more likely than whites to be told that a job had been filled when a subsequent white applicant was invited for an interview. The study provided strong evidence that racial discrimination significantly reduced the labor-market opportunities of blacks in Toronto, and it received wide coverage in the media.

---

16 The terms "institutional discrimination" and "systemic discrimination" are in frequent use. Institutional or systemic discrimination is discrimination that occurs for reasons other than the racial attitudes of individual employers. This form of discrimination may be direct or indirect.

Henry (1989) conducted a replication of the 1984 field trials (Henry and Ginsberg 1985) in 1989. The Economic Council of Canada argued that the new study showed "dramatic change," in that "there was now no racial discrimination in job offers based on face-to-face interviews" (Swan et al. 1991, 118). However, the demand for labor in Toronto was much greater in 1989 than it had been in 1984, and heavy labor demand often temporarily improves the opportunities for disadvantaged groups. The Economic Council maintained that "the tight labour market in Toronto cannot account in any obvious direct way for the 1989 results: the employers who were tested had the possibility of choosing between equally qualified blacks and whites" (ibid.). Thus, "employers have gradually become more tolerant, just like the rest of Canadians" (ibid.). This argument is not convincing. The research procedure specified that the black applicants approach the employers first. In a tight labor market, employers are likely to hire the first qualified applicant who comes along. In nearly half of the 1989 field-trial cases in which a black was hired, the offer was made "on the spot," before the white had a chance to apply (Henry 1989, 19–20). When these cases are removed from the analysis (to eliminate the effect of the strong labor demand), the results show that more job offers were made to whites than to blacks, and that no statistically significant change had occurred since 1984.[17] The research procedure appears to have given the black applicant an advantage in 1989 that may have offset employer bias (see Reitz 1993, 1994). Nevertheless, like the 1984 study, the 1989 study found many indications of discriminatory treatment (Henry 1989, 24–29).

Field trials in Washington, DC, and Chicago (Turner, Fix, and Struyk 1991) showed levels of discrimination comparable to those that Henry and Ginsberg found in Toronto in 1984. The study was undertaken to evaluate what its conductors describe as a belief — used as a basis for judicial and administrative decisionmaking — that, because of American progress in combating discrimination, the

---

17 The results showed less racial difference in 1989 than in 1984, but because of the small size of the two studies the evidence of change over time might be attributable to chance (with a probability greater than one in twenty).

country is "well on the way to becoming a color-blind society" (Turner, Fix, and Struyk 1991, 1). They refer to "some scholars who claim that most overt discrimination has been eliminated and... others who argue that the residual is not worthy of elimination by state coercion" (ibid.). In the US study, whites received three times as many job offers as blacks (Turner, Fix, and Struyk 1991, 19). They were also three times as likely to be invited for a job interview. "If equally qualified black and white candidates are in competition for a job, when differential treatment occurs, it is three times more likely to favor the white applicant over the black" (Turner, Fix, and Struyk 1991, 32). Differential treatment was somewhat greater in the Washington trials than in those conducted in Chicago.

The similarity between the results of the 1984 Henry and Ginsberg study and those of the Turner, Fix, and Struyk study suggests that discriminatory practices are not widely different in the two countries. The Economic Council of Canada's view that a form of racial discrimination of comparable importance in the two countries disappeared — in one country but not in the other — in a few years should not be accepted without a clear explanation of how it happened in such a short time.

Collective and Government Action against Discrimination

Americans have at times regarded race relations as one of their country's leading problems, a perception that has led to pressure for government action. A poll conducted in 1963, after a decade of growing racial unrest, showed that 52 percent of the US population considered racial problems to be the most important facing the country; only 25 percent gave priority to the threat of war with the Soviet Union. Later, the prominence of the race issue receded, but it continues to be more significant in the United States than it has ever been in Canada (Michalos 1982, 189–201).

In the context of race, accordingly, Americans have been more likely than Canadians to favor government action. In 1970, 25 percent of Americans, but only 11 percent of Canadians, put "reducing racial discrimination" among the top three government priorities for the future (Michalos 1982, 202). And, of course, the US government has indeed taken more action (Jain and Sloane 1981; Jain 1989). The Canadian federal government has avoided US-style legislation to mandate equal employment, on the ground that the problem is less serious in Canada (Reitz 1988b).

The higher priority that Americans have placed on racial discrimination is attributable in part to the higher level of racial conflict in the United States; it does not necessarily indicate a greater underlying predisposition to favor government action against discrimination. Indeed, as racial conflict has declined, Americans' willingness to invoke government action against discrimination seems to have declined somewhat as well, even though racial tolerance has increased. Table 7 shows that, even as racial attitudes and social-distance scores improved in the 1970s and 1980s, whites became more supportive of policies to assist blacks only in the area of housing and accommodations, and less supportive of such policies in other areas, including schools.

Kluegel (1990) uses GSS data for 1986, 1988, and 1989 to probe Americans' attitudes toward assisting blacks to achieve equality. The GSS respondents were asked the following:

> Some people think that blacks have been discriminated against for so long that the government has a special obligation to help improve their living standards. Others believe that the government should not be giving special treatment to blacks....Where would you place yourself on this scale, or haven't you made up your mind on this?

Pooling the surveys, Kluegel finds that only 13.8 percent agreed that the government was obligated to help blacks; 59.3 percent stated that the government had no such obligation, and 26.9 percent took a position in between. Pooled analysis of these surveys, plus others conducted in 1977 and 1985, showed that the US population was evenly split between those who thought the government was doing too much — 26.8 percent — and those who thought it was doing too little — 24.7 percent.[18] Kluegel makes this point:

> The only substantial change between 1977 and the late 1980s in how whites view the black-white socio-economic gap is a decline in the attribution of that gap to inborn ability differences. This decline parallels the trend of declining traditional prejudice.... The abatement of perhaps the most invidious explanation for the black-white status gap has not been accompanied by any noteworthy increase in attributions that favor efforts to provide equal opportunity for black Americans. (Kluegel 1990, 523.)

Smith's (1990, 7) analysis of the 1990 GSS data shows that negative images of blacks in the context of work and welfare have had a direct effect on support for affirmative action for blacks. Thus, although the explanations that Americans give for racial disadvantages have changed, there is a persistent reluctance to identify discrimination as a major cause of these disadvantages, and hence resistance to policies intended to offset discrimination. Bobo (1988, 109) offers a group-conflict interpretation of this resistance, suggesting that whites oppose "change that might impose substantial burdens on whites."

In Canada, no survey has asked if the government has an obligation to secure equal opportunity for blacks. The 1987 Charter Study,[19] however, did ask respondents if the government has an obligation to ensure equal opportunity in general. The statement "while equal opportunity to succeed is important for all Canadians, it's not really the government's job to guarantee it" elicited agreement from 63.3 percent of the respondents and disagreement from 33.7 percent. By contrast, as we noted above, only 13.8 percent of Americans approved of government intervention to assist blacks. Of course, Canadian opinions might be different if racial minorities were targeted as beneficiaries. Support for government action to

---

18 The overall results reported here are recalculated from Kluegel's (1990, 521, table 5).

19 A survey of attitudes to the Canadian Charter of Rights and Freedoms is described in Sniderman et al. 1991. We are grateful to Joseph Fletcher for providing data from this survey reported below.

ensure equal opportunity might not translate into support for government action to assist a particular group.

Sniderman and Hagen (1985) show that American rejection of government intervention is linked to "individualism," and suggest that individualist values militate against collective solutions. If this is true, then Canadians, who are less committed to individualism than Americans are, may be more willing to support government intervention. However, the causal relation between values and policy may work the other way: opposition to government assistance to blacks may reinforce individualism, which, in turn, may be invoked to legitimate racial inequality.

Thus, although discrimination has been a bigger political issue in the United States than it has been in Canada, and although more government intervention has occurred in the United States, Americans are not more likely than Canadians to favor collective responses to discrimination. Given their greater individualism, they may be less likely. Earlier, we showed that Canadians and Americans seem to be equally uncomfortable with the idea that discrimination is an explanation for inequality. The fact that social distances are less great in Canada may not mean that Canadians are more open to government intervention to ensure racial equality.

Summary

The findings reviewed here suggest that, despite the historical differences between race relations in Canada and race relations in the United States, Canadians and Americans are roughly similar in their attitudes and behavior toward racial minorities. In both countries, blatant racism is marginal and the social distance between racial minorities and other groups is diminishing. The incidence of anti-Semitic attitudes and behavior is about the same in each country, and so is the incidence of discrimination in employment. A majority of both Canadians and Americans feel that minorities are responsible for their own inequality, that discrimination is not a major cause of inequality, and that government should not intervene to ensure equality.

Although the social distance between the majority and the racial minorities has declined in both countries, it has consistently been smaller in Canada, especially in relation to intermarriage. Depending on the dimension of social distance in question, Canadian attitudes may be either comparable to American attitudes or a decade or more ahead of them.

One likely reason the social distance between the races is greater in the United States is that economic distance is greater as well — a point we shall discuss in Chapter 5. Another likely reason is that racial minorities constitute a much larger proportion of the total population in the United States than they do in Canada. Thus there may be a sense among white Americans that exclusion is necessary to maintain a degree of racial homogeneity that white Canadians take for granted.

The cross-national differences in social distance do not seem to produce significant differences between the two countries in regard to racial stereotyping, racial discrimination in employment and other important areas, the perception of discrimination as a cause of inequality, or willingness to support government intervention to oppose discrimination. Nor does the decline in social distance over time in both countries seem to have produced much change in any of these other matters. More research is needed on the impact of social values on attitudes and behavior toward racial minorities. Individualism in the United States may work against the adoption of public policies such as affirmative action. But Canadians, too, have been extremely reluctant to adopt such policies and, in fact, have adopted fewer of them. To the extent that Americans differ from Canadians by emphasizing equality of opportunity over equality of result, and to the extent that Canadians exhibit less religious traditionalism than Americans do, there may be greater tolerance of social diversity in Canada. However, the impact of these factors on the treatment of racial minorities in areas such as employment or government policy has yet to be demonstrated.

Chapter 5

The Economic Incorporation of Minorities

How well are ethnic and racial minorities in Canada and the United States incorporated into the mainstream institutions of their respective societies? In this chapter, we shall focus on the position of immigrants, especially those of non-European background. We shall look at social mobility, measured in terms of earnings from employment, and ask whether recent immigrants, many of whom have non-European backgrounds, have had comparable employment experiences in the two countries. Our analysis will review the results of other studies and take a fresh look at some relevant Canadian and US census data.

The results of any inquiry into the status of immigrant groups will depend, of course, on the researcher's choice of a benchmark group — that is, on what group the researcher uses to represent the mainstream standard. For both the United States and Canada outside Quebec, one appropriate benchmark group would be persons of English or, at least, British origin. Some of the studies we discuss here use this group as the benchmark. Others use a broader category, such as "unhyphenated whites" (Lieberson 1985) or, if it is the status of racial minorities that is under scrutiny, whites in general. A few studies use British immigrants. For Quebec, both the French majority and the English minority are appropriate benchmark groups. In the case of minority women, the benchmark implied by standard employment analyses, which consider men and women separately, is majority-group women. However, given that this group is itself at a disadvantage in the labor market, it may be more appropriate to use majority males as the benchmark for both minority men and minority women. Some researchers have adopted this procedure. In any case, our cross-national comparisons will have to take variations in the definition of the benchmark group into account.

The studies use two key measures of socio-economic incorporation: (1) the overall disparity in occupational status or earnings between the immigrant group and the benchmark group, and (2) the disparity in status or earnings that remains after adjustments have been made for differences between the groups in job qualifications such as education, language skills, and work experience. Both components have social significance. Some analysts, however, emphasize the importance of adjusted or "net" disparities, arguing that any disparity that remains after adjustment must be attributable to a racial or ethnic discrimination. Others dispute this conclusion and point to other possible causes of the remaining disparity.

We shall present both the overall and the net results of the various studies we consider. Having done that, we shall ask whether net disparity in earnings or occupational status is a valid measure of economic discrimination. The issue is the extent to which employment discrimination in each country, which we examined in Chapter 4, creates disparities in the relative occupational status or earnings of immigrant minority groups. The hypothesis of Canadian tolerance implies that discrimination will produce greater disparities in status or earnings for racial minority immigrants in the United States. We shall consider comparative data on the economic incorporation of these immigrants in terms of their implications for this hypothesis.

Background:
Race in the United States
and Language in Canada

One might hope to address the question of the comparative incorporation of minority groups by examining the most important historical instances of incorporation in the two countries — namely, the experiences of American blacks and French-Canadians. As we argued in Chapter 1, however, so many confounding factors and conditions have affected the positions of these groups that their current circumstances are anything but simple reflections of the social forces that are assumed to operate in the American melting pot and the Canadian mosaic.

Nevertheless, it will be useful to consider the occupational positions of immigrants in Canada and the United States in relation to the occupational positions of the major minority groups. The continuing impact of race on occupational status in the United States is a benchmark of disadvantage against which one can measure the position of immigrants in both countries. The occupational position of French-Canadians, by contrast, is not useful. Many of the most important processes of incorporation that affect French-Canadians occur at the level of the collectivity, and are therefore quite different from those that affect immigrants.

The Mobility of African-Americans

The following is a brief sketch of the occupational mobility and current position of American blacks. Gunnar Myrdal's *An American Dilemma* (1944) is the classic scholarly account of the historical gap between the American ideal of equal opportunity and the reality of racial inequality. Myrdal described how black-white relations evolved from slave system to caste system to class system, and how educated and culturally assimilated blacks became embittered by continued exclusion from white society. He showed how black protest movements had consistently failed to produce meaningful change. And he predicted increasing conflict if the inequalities continued. The explosion of racial conflict in the 1960s confirmed in grim fashion both the accuracy of Myrdal's analysis and his failure to convince American whites of the need for significant change.

Although racial conflict produced policy responses in the 1960s, steady improvements in the position of blacks had been under way for some time. Between 1940 and 1980, black male wages increased from 43.3 percent to 72.6 percent of white male wages (Smith and Welch 1989; Smith 1984). Increases were fastest in the 1940s and slowest in the 1950s. Improvements in the 1960s and 1970s — often, though not without controversy, attributed to affirmative action programs — benefited young and highly educated blacks most (see also Featherman and Hauser 1978). Smith and Welch (1989, 558) attribute about half of the postwar black gains to general economic growth and half to improvements in black education, improvements that occurred both because blacks migrated to the North and because Southern schools improved.

Carlson and Swartz (1988, 543) show that the relative earnings of blacks, both men and women, improved between 1959 and 1979, especially after adjustment for education and other demographic variables.[1] The geometric mean earnings of black men increased from 54.7 percent to 65.1 percent of the earnings of white men. After adjustments, the increase was from 74.8 percent to 84.5 percent. For black women, the analysis was limited to the period 1969 to 1979. Geometric mean earnings increased from 33.2 percent to 43.3 percent of the earnings of white men. After adjustment, they increased from 50.7 percent to 64.9 percent (Carlson and Swartz 1988, 543; see also Farley 1983, 1984; Allen and Farley 1986; Farley and Allen 1987).

The mean earnings of black women actually achieved equality with those of white women in 1979. White and black women earned 44 and 43.3 percent, respectively, of white male earnings. After adjustment for education and other variables, they earned 62.8 and 64.9 percent, respectively. However, Blau and Beller (1988, 523) show that a sample selection bias distorts this comparison (see Heckman 1979). Pressures to enter the labor force increased more rapidly for white women and induced them increasingly to accept lower wage offers. When the earnings data are corrected for selection bias, black women are in fact disadvantaged relative to white women, as well as relative to black and white men.

---

1 The demographic variables include years of education and its square, variables representing six age categories (18–24, 25–34, 34–44, 45–54, 55–64, and 65+), an estimate of hours worked during the year (usual hours worked per week times the number of weeks worked), marital status, birthplace, whether English was used at home, and three variables representing residence (in Washington DC, Hawaii, and the South); see Carlson and Swartz 1988, 532.

These figures suggest that the full incorporation of American blacks into mainstream society is still a long way off. Oliver and Glick (1982, 518) argue on the basis of mobility data from 1962 and 1973 that "blacks, even with their improved rates of mobility, and even after 10 generations, will not attain the occupational distribution of whites in 1962."

Some analysts argue that even the improvements seen in the statistical averages are partially illusory. William Julius Wilson, in *The Declining Significance of Race* (1978), argues that, although the black middle class has grown, inequality *within* the black population is increasing. There is still a black "underclass" that is not participating in the general upward trend (see also Wilson 1987). This situation has been exacerbated by economic restructuring and employment shifts away from "rustbelt" cities. Sharon Collins (1983) points to the political and budgetary vulnerability of black employment in government, which increased from 12 percent of total employment in government in 1960 to 23 percent in 1982.

In the 1980s — the Reagan years — the trends again became less favorable. There were apparently no further improvements in earnings for blacks; indeed, there may have been a reversal, particularly for younger males. This state of affairs compounds a decline in black employment. An increase in income inequality in the United States during the 1980s affected blacks most, particularly black men (Grubb and Wilson 1989, 5–7). The slowing or halting of black improvement is clear in the National Academy of Sciences study *A Common Destiny* (Jaynes and Williams 1989; see also Harris and Wilkins 1988). Noting that "the greatest economic gains for blacks occurred in the 1940s and 1960s," the study concluded that, "since the early 1970s, the economic status of blacks relative to whites has, on the average, stagnated or deteriorated....Some blacks have attained high-status occupations, income, education, and political position, but a substantial minority remain in disadvantaged circumstances" (Jaynes and Williams 1989, 6). The gains were attributable to improvements in the legal status of blacks and other government actions and programs, and to the buoyancy of the economy; the causes of the subsequent stagnation have been resistance to change by white Americans and the economic slowdown since 1973.

In sum, although American blacks have moved up over time, they continue to face very substantial disadvantages. Racial conflict declined after the mid-1970s, but disparities between blacks and whites remain. The Carlson and Swartz data (1988, 543) indicate that black men still earn only about 65 to 70 percent of what white men earn — 80 to 85 percent after adjustments for education and human capital. Black women earn less than half of what white men earn — perhaps tow-thirds as much after adjustments.

French-English Relations in Canada

French-Canadians constitute just under 30 percent of the population of Canada but 82 percent of the population of Quebec. About three French-Canadians in four reside in Quebec. Therefore, the incorporation of French-Canadians into Canadian society is to a significant degree a reflection of the position of Quebec within Canada, as well as of the position of French-Canadians as individuals within Quebec and throughout the rest of Canada.

We should emphasize that the employment mobility of French-Canadians is not a sufficient measure of the incorporation of the group as a whole, or of its incorporation relative to that of African-Americans. The incorporation of French-Canadians into Canadian society has political, cultural, linguistic, and socio-economic dimensions. Employment mobility is only one of many components and it is one of decreasing or even vanishing political significance.

French-Canadians' disadvantages in the sphere of employment are much less severe today within Quebec and across Canada than they were in 1965, when Porter described them in *The Vertical Mosaic*. In the Quiet Revolution of the 1950s and 1960s, French-Canadian educational levels, occupational status, and incomes all moved up. In 1961, the earnings of French-Canadian men were about 78 percent of the earnings of Canadian men of British origin, a figure lower than those for many other groups of European origin in Canada (Breton,

Reitz, and Valentine 1980, 148). By 1981, this proportion had increased to 90 percent, and French-Canadian women had only slightly lower earnings than did women of British origin; in relation to levels of education, French-Canadians experienced no disadvantages at all (Li 1988, 88, 116). Within Quebec, the minority anglophone community has always enjoyed a comparative advantage, but this too has declined, and in relation to levels of education and other human capital it has disappeared. In 1970, unilingual anglophones in Quebec earned 59 percent more than unilingual francophones; in 1980, 22 percent more. If these figures are adjusted for education and other human capital, the advantage is actually with francophones (Vaillancourt 1989, 84–87).

Immigrants of European Origin

Despite difficulties and conflicts, the story of European immigration in both Canada and the United States is largely a success story. The descendants of European immigrants in the United States have achieved occupational and earnings equality with the benchmark group, and those in Canada have either done so or are in the process of doing so.

The study of the 1980 US census by Lieberson and Waters (1988) provides a comprehensive assessment of the occupational and earnings position of native-born Americans of European descent. Americans of English descent constitute the largest and oldest of the European groups, and so for most analysts they provide the benchmark against which to measure the status of the other group.[2] However, most of the other European groups also consist primarily of at least third-generation descendants of immigrants, and for most of the largest the proportion of at least third-generation Americans is 90 percent or more (Lieberson and Waters 1988, 45).

---

2 The sizes of the major European ancestry groups in the United States are as follows: English, 21.9 percent of the total population; German, 21.7 percent; Irish, 17.7 percent; French, 5.7 percent; Italian, 5.4 percent; Scottish, 4.4 percent; Polish, 3.6 percent; and Dutch, 2.8 percent (Lieberson and Waters 1988, 34).

Although the European immigrants encountered disadvantage as well as opportunity, their descendants have achieved a degree of educational, occupational, and income mobility comparable to that of the native-born population of English origin. This generalization applies to women as well as to men, though the gender gap varies somewhat by ethnic group. Lieberson and Waters (1988, 155) sum up as follows:

> Socioeconomic inequalities among white ethnic groups are both relatively minor and unrelated to patterns of ethnic inequality found earlier in the century. The once major differences among specific white groups as well as the old-new distinction in occupation and income are largely gone. The differences which do continue for these groups are...rather subtle.

The impact of race on the earnings of the native-born is, as we have shown, far more dramatic than the impact of European origins. American blacks experience inequality and inequality of opportunity, but Americans of European origin find full equality (see also Greeley 1976; Jiobu 1990).

Comparative analysis for Canada of the economic incorporation of groups of European origin must take account of Canada's more recent immigration history. Porter's (1965) evidence that groups of European origin in Canada were disadvantaged by ethnic isolation did not take into account the impact on earnings of low education and lack of fluency in English or French. Subsequent more detailed analysis has shown that, when levels of education are taken into account, people of European origins, like their American counterparts, are not disadvantaged. For example, the occupational status and earnings of Canadians of Italian descent are relatively low, but so is their level of education. With appropriate adjustments, the position of the various European groups — and this applies to both men and women — appears to be on a par with the position of the English-Canadian benchmark group (see Kalback 1970; Darroch 1979; Reitz 1980a; 1980b; 1990; Li 1988).

The evidence is fairly clear: the European-immigration success story might be told with equal enthusiasm in both Canada and the

United States. The main difference is that, in the United States, the story is essentially over, whereas in Canada, it is still unfolding. All of the indications are that, in Canada, contrary to Porter's metaphor of the "vertical mosaic," immigrant opportunity is a reality for immigrants from Europe. Moreover, equality of opportunity in the United States does not imply that assimilation is more rapid there than it is in Canada; as Chapter 3 has shown, there is no consistent difference between the two countries in this regard.

Immigrants of Non-European Origin

Recent non-European immigration has had a significant demographic impact in many major cities in the United States, and in most major cities in Canada. In the United States, persons of Hispanic origin, including principally Mexican-Americans, Cuban-Americans, and Puerto Ricans, and also including Hispanics of European origin, accounted for 6 percent of the population in 1980 and 9.5 percent in 1992 (Lieberson and Waters 1988, 34; US Bureau of the Census 1989, 49; O'Hare 1992, 10). Persons of Asian origin account for about 3 percent. Black immigration is also significant; most black immigrants are from the Caribbean (some are Hispanic), but some are from Africa.

The demographic impact of immigration is greater in Canada and, as in the United States, the racial composition of immigration is changing; consequently, non-European groups account for a rapidly growing proportion of the Canadian population as well. By 1986, 6 percent of the adult population were members of the so-called "visible minorities," and nearly 90 percent of these adults were foreign-born. Immigrant members of racial minorities account for a substantial proportion of total population — up to nearly 20 percent — in major immigrant-reception areas such as Toronto. Asians are the largest racial minority group, and Chinese immigrants and their descendants are the largest Asian group. The Asian and black Caribbean groups are proportionately somewhat larger in Canada than they are in the United States. In contrast to the United States,

Canada has received comparatively few Hispanic immigrants. So our main comparisons of the two countries will be for Asian and black immigrants.

Relative Educational Levels

Immigrants in the United States have on average less education, relative to the native-born, than do immigrants in Canada. Borjas (1988, 43) has shown that foreign-born males in the United States in 1980 had on average 1 year less education than the native-born, whereas foreign-born males in Canada in 1981 had on average 0.4 years *more* education than the native-born; the cross-national difference for females is comparable. The generalization that the relative educational levels of immigrants are lower in the United States holds across most of the major origin groups, but the extent of the difference varies. It is greatest in the case of immigrants of Latin-American origin, mainly because the average level of education among Mexican immigrants in the United States is very low. Latin-American immigrants in the United States have on average 3.3 years less education than native-born Americans, whereas Latin-American immigrants in Canada have on average 0.8 years *more* education than native-born Canadians. The cross-national difference is much smaller in the case of Asian immigrants. In both countries, the Asian-born are better-educated than the native-born, but whereas the Asian-born in the United States have 1.9 years more education than the native-born, the Asian-born in Canada have 2.3 years more education.

The difference between the two countries in this regard is probably attributable in great part to the fact that the educational level of the native-born is higher in the United States. In 1980, the average native-born American male in the adult labor force had 12.7 years of education, whereas the comparable Canadian had 11.3 years, a difference of 1.33 years.[3] At that time, foreign-born adult labor force males in the two countries had the same average level of

---

3 These averages are based on census data that are not fully comparable, owing to differences between the census questions on education. However, the essential point of the comparison is valid.

education, 11.7 years (Borjas 1988, 43). Thus, the average immigrant in the United States is a full year less well-educated than the native-born, whereas similar immigrants in Canada are better educated than the native-born by almost half a year. Americans have more educational credentials than Canadians, a circumstance that makes the competitive position of immigrants more difficult in the United States.

Chiswick (1978, 1986) and Borjas (1985) show that, in fact, rising educational standards in the United States seem to coincide with a widening education gap between immigrants and native-born Americans. The level of education of the native-born US labor force has risen for all racial groups. For example, between 1970 and 1980, the average schooling of adult native-born white men rose from 11.9 to 13.1 years, an increase of 1.2 years (Chiswick 1986, 180).[4] Immigrant education levels rose less rapidly. For immigrants in the country in 1980, the mean level of education for those who had arrived between 1975 and 1980 was 12.3 years, little different from the mean of 12.2 years for those who had arrived between 1950 and 1964.

The level of education of a country's immigrant population depends in part on the country's immigrant selection policy. Thus, Borjas (1990) argues that the greater educational disadvantage of US immigrants may be attributable to differences between Canadian immigration policy and US policy; that is, Canada may in general give more weight to educational criteria than the United States does (see also Briggs 1984; Chiswick 1988; Simon 1989). There are in fact differences in immigration policy (see Boyd 1976; Reimers and Troper 1992) that have likely had some effect on the difference between the levels of immigrant educational disadvantage in the two countries. However, with the exception of immigrants from Latin America, immigrants to the United States are generally *better* educated than immigrants to Canada. It does not seem to be the case, therefore, that Canadian immigration practice is more selective on

---

4 The major native-born minority groups gained even more. Native-born black men gained 1.5 years in education (rising from 9.9 years to 11.6), native-born Mexicans gained 2 years (rising from 8.9 years to 10.9), and native-born Chinese gained 2.3 years (rising from 12.7 years to 15).

educational grounds than US immigration practice. Consequently, differences in immigration policy or practice are not likely to be the major cause of the circumstance that the immigrant-education gap is larger in the United States than it is in Canada.

Relative Earnings

The cross-national differences in the relative educational levels of immigrants are important in determining the cross-national differences in relative earnings. However, most analyses of immigrant earnings, in both countries, have emphasized the earnings disadvantages of immigrants net of relative educational levels.[5] They have taken immigrant educational levels as given. These studies find that, in both countries, non-European immigrants earn substantially less than they would be expected to earn on the basis of their job qualifications, such as education, knowledge of English (or French), and work experience. This is true whether the benchmark group is native-born whites or immigrants from Europe.

In both countries, the generalization that non-European immigrants are disadvantaged applies to both men and women. The data and the earnings analyses for women, however, have been less detailed than those for men. Variation in levels of labor force participation and patterns of employment among women in different minority groups introduces difficult problems for earnings analysis (Carlson and Swartz 1988). It is clear, however, that race and gender interact to affect earnings in both countries.[6] Immigrant women in both countries are handicapped by a lack of knowledge of the language of the host society (Boyd 1992a). Geschwender (1991) has shown that labor force participation by women varies with ethnic origin in both

---

5 For the United States, see Borjas 1985; Chiswick 1978, 1986; Reimers 1983; Bean and Tienda 1987; and Model 1991. For Canada, see Goldlust and Richmond 1973; Li 1988; Reitz 1980b, 1988, 1990; de Silva 1992; Boyd 1992b; Christofides and Swidinsky 1994.

6 For the United States, see Stier 1991; Cooney and Ortiz 1991; and Hughey 1990. For Canada, see Verma and Basavarajappa 1989; Reitz 1990; Boyd 1986; 1992b; Christofides and Swidinsky 1994. For a cross-national comparison, see Geschwender 1991.

countries. In particular, he shows that high labor force participation by married women of Chinese origin in both countries helped to offset the disadvantage experienced by men in Chinese families.

Our key question is the extent to which racial-minority immigrant disadvantage varies between the two countries. Borjas (1988, 1990), Chiswick (1986, 1988), and Nakamura and Nakamura (1992) have all used 1980 US and 1981 Canadian census data to examine the earnings of recent male immigrants in Canada and the United States, overall and by birthplace groupings. Borjas (1990, 208–210) shows that the earnings of male immigrants relative to the earnings of native-born males have been higher in Canada. If one adjusts for relative levels of education and other demographic characteristics, however, virtually no cross-national difference remains. The projected lifetime earnings of immigrants who entered the United States during the five-year period before the 1980 census were about 30 percent less than those of the native-born; for Canada, the comparable figure was only 10 percent. After adjustment for demographic characteristics, however, the disadvantage was about 20 percent in both countries. For immigrants born in Asia, the adjusted difference between earnings in Canada and earnings in the United States was small (Borjas 1988, 51 and 67; see also Nakamura and Nakamura 1992, 162–163).

Chiswick's analysis of earnings in the United States uses more detailed birthplace groups than Borjas' does and therefore permits a better assessment of racial origins.[7] His benchmark group is immigrants from the United Kingdom.[8] Male immigrants from the

---

7 Most immigrants from Africa in both countries are not black, and immigrants from Latin America in the United States include a large number of illegal Mexican immigrants, which is not at all the case in Canada.

8 As Chiswick (1986, 178) explains, "The natural logarithm of earnings is regressed on a set of country-of-birth dichotomous variables with immigrants from the United Kingdom serving as a benchmark. For small differences the country regression coefficient approximates the percentage difference in earnings, but not for large differences. The country coefficients...have been converted to relative differences by computing one minus the antilog of the regression coefficient. When multiplied by 100, it is the percentage difference in earnings."

West Indies (mostly black), Vietnam (mostly refugees), and Mexico and elsewhere in Latin America (except Cuba), earn about half the amounts earned by UK immigrants. The members of all other non-European immigrant groups, except South Asians, earn between 32 and 39 percent less than UK immigrants earn; South Asians earn about 24 percent less. Non-European immigrants' lower levels of education or other human capital partially explain the lower earnings. But the differences between demographically comparable groups of non-European and UK immigrants are less extreme. If adjustments are made for years of schooling, experience, weeks worked, marital status, and geographic area, then immigrants from the West Indies, most of Asia, and Mexico and elsewhere in Latin America earn about 30 percent less than immigrants from the United Kingdom; immigrants from South Asia, "other Asia," and the Middle East earn about 15 to 17 percent less.[9]

Chiswick's (1988, 187) Canadian analysis unfortunately identifies only one non-European origin category: Asian birthplace. Canadian immigrants of Asian birth earned 36 percent less than UK immigrants, 18 percent less after demographic adjustment. This suggests that, for Asians, net inequalities are significantly less in Canada than they are in the United States, where many Asian groups earned between 15 and 29 percent less than UK immigrants, after adjustment. However, because of the diversity of the experiences of specific Asian-origin groups in the two countries, the comparison is not a straightforward one.

Chiswick's US data can be more usefully compared with the more complete analysis of the earnings of non-European immigrants in Canada, based on 1981 census data, in Verma and Basavarajappa (1989, 457–8). Caribbean immigrant males earned 12 percent less than native-born Canadians, immigrants from Southeast Asia (in-

---

9 Chiswick (1986, 177) attributes most of the disadvantage of Mexicans and Puerto Ricans to low levels of education. However, the adjustment for the very low average levels of education of Mexican immigrants is doubtful, since the white native-born population with comparably low levels of education is too small to serve as a standard.

cluding Vietnamese) earned 10 percent less, and immigrants from East Asia (many of them Chinese) earned 6 percent less.

In order to compare these Canadian data with Chiswick's US data, account must be taken of Chiswick's UK-immigrant benchmark. The adjustment is an easy one, since Verma and Basavarajappa report UK-immigrant earnings. Table 11 presents figures based on the UK benchmark for both countries, using approximately comparable birthplace groups. For immigrants from the West Indies, South Asia, Southeast Asia, and East Asia, the unadjusted earnings disadvantages are much greater in the United States; after adjustment for demographic differences, however, the earnings disadvantages in the two countries are within 4 percentage points of one another. For immigrants from the West Indies and East Asia, the disadvantages are greater in the United States. For immigrants from South Asia and Southeast Asia, they are greater in Canada.[10]

It is worth comparing the degrees of disadvantage reflected in these data with the data for African-Americans summarized earlier. If one adjusts for educational and demographic differences, African-American males earned about 20 percent less than white males. The data from Verma and Basavarajappa for the earnings of Caribbean male immigrants to Canada — 21 percent less than the earnings of native-born Canadians, 25 percent less than the earnings of UK immigrants — reflect a roughly similar degree of disadvantage. Relative to education, black immigrants in Canada do not earn more than do native-born American blacks. Chiswick's US data for West Indian male immigrants — 30 percent less earnings than UK immigrants — also reflect a roughly similar degree of disadvantage, given a similar relative position for UK immigrants. In an analysis of 1980 US census data, Model (1991) shows that, relative to education, blacks from the Caribbean do not, overall, have higher earnings than native-born African-Americans, though the earnings of some Caribbean groups are higher.

---

10 For additional analysis of the earnings disadvantages of racial-minority immigrants in relation to levels of education, see Basavarajappa and Verma 1985; Beaujot, Basavarajappa, and Verma 1988; and Statistics Canada 1992.

Table 11: Earnings[a] of Selected Groups of Male Immigrants to the United States and Canada Relative to Earnings of UK-Born Male Immigrants, 1980 and 1981[b]

1980 US Data (from Chiswick 1986)			1981 Canadian Data (from Verma and Basavarajappa 1989)		
	Relative Earnings[c]			Relative Earnings[d]	
Birthplace	Overall	Net	Birthplace	Overall	Net
South Asia	− 0.24	− 0.15	South Asia	+ 0.02	− 0.19
China	− 0.39	− 0.29	East Asia	− 0.11	− 0.25
West Indies	− 0.47	− 0.30	Caribbean	− 0.16	− 0.25
Vietnam	− 0.50	− 0.26	Southeast Asia	− 0.14	− 0.30

[a] Both studies report wage and salary employment earnings, including self-employment earnings.

[b] Chiswick's sample consists of males aged 25–64, with nonzero earnings in the preceding year; the sample is drawn from the 1980 US public use microdata C file, 1/100 sample. Verma and Basavarajappa's sample consists of males aged 15+ who worked full time for 40+ weeks and had nonzero earnings in the preceding year; the sample is drawn from the 20 percent sample of households.

[c] Chiswick's data are based on regression analyses of the natural logarithm of earnings. The table note (Chiswick 1986, 187) states that "the parameter reported is one minus the antilog of the country of origin regression coefficient. When multiplied by 100 it is the percent difference in earnings. The benchmark is immigrants from the United Kingdom." In the net earnings figures, the control variables are period of immigration, education, experience, experience squared, weeks worked, urban/rural, south/nonsouth, and marital status.

[d] Verma and Basavarajappa's data are differences in the mean and adjusted differences derived by a technique of direct standardization. The overall earnings of the UK-born immigrants are 117.8 percent of the earnings of the Canadian-born; after adjustments, they are 104.4 percent of the earnings of the Canadian-born. The overall figures are based on national data; the net figures are for persons living in a census metropolitan area, and are adjusted for age and education.

Sources: Chiswick 1986, 187 (United States); Verma and Basavarajappa 1989, 457–458 (Canada).

For a more precise comparison, one should use comparable racial categories, use a sample that has been selected in comparable ways in the two countries, and include women as well as men. To accomplish these objectives, we have prepared a sample based on the 1980 US census and the 1981 Canadian census. The sample includes two groups of recent immigrants whose race is identified clearly in both censuses: blacks and Chinese. In the US data, both groups are treated as races, though of course "Chinese" is a nationality rather than a race. In the Canadian data, they are treated as ethnic groups, even though "black" signifies a race rather than an ethnic origin. Our sample consists of recent immigrants in these two groups — that is, immigrants who had arrived within the preceding 10 years — and native-born whites. The sample is restricted to the adult urban labor force.[11] Although the two immigrant groups account for fewer than 20 percent of the recent urban immigrants in each country, they are large enough for the purposes of our comparison.

Table 12 shows the results of our analysis. For both black and Chinese immigrants, the education gap with native-born whites is greater in the United States than it is in Canada. On average, black male immigrants in the United States report 12.2 years of education, whereas black male immigrants in Canada report 11.9 years. But whereas black male immigrants in the United States have on average 1.2 years less education than native-born white males, black male immigrants in Canada are as well-educated as native-born white males. Similar remarks apply to the other race and gender categories.

Table 12 also shows that the earnings of recent black male immigrants to the United States are about 46 percent lower than the earnings of native-born white males, and that the earnings of recent Chinese male immigrants are about 37 percent lower.[12] After adjustment, these numbers drop to 33 percent in each case. Canadian black and Chinese immigrants have relatively higher earnings than their counterparts in the United States: their earnings disadvantages are only 31 percent and 23 percent, respectively. After adjustment, however, these figures rise to 33 percent and 27 percent. The difference

---

11 Canadian data come from the 1981 Public Use Sample Tape, 2 percent individual file. US data come from the 1980 Public Use Microdata Sample, 5 percent A Sample. In each case, the subsample consists of all members of the labor force aged 16–64 who live in urban areas with populations greater than 500,000 and earn at least $100 per year.

12 The results in Table 12 are based on regression analyses of the pooled US-Canadian samples; pooled-sample regressions permit statistical tests of cross-national differences. For clarity of presentation, however, the table reports immigrant earnings as a proportion of the earnings of native-born in each country.

Table 12: Comparison of Education and Earnings[a] of Recent Chinese and Black Immigrants to the United States and Canada, 1980–81, Pooled Sample[b]

Group	Mean Years of Education	Earnings 1980 US $	Earnings Relative to Native-Born White Earnings Overall[c]		Earnings Relative to Native-Born White Earnings Net[d]		Number in Sample
Males, United States							
Native-born white	13.4	18,438					125,664
Chinese immigrant, 1970–80	13.2	11,658	− 0.37	**	− 0.33	**	3,508
Black immigrant, 1970–80	12.2	10,010	− 0.46	**	− 0.33	**	5,011
Males, Canada							
Native-born white	11.9	14,599					2,064
Chinese immigrant, 1971–81	12.7	11,176	− 0.23	++	− 0.27	+	658
Black immigrant, 1971–81	11.9	10,113	− 0.31	+	− 0.33	n.s.	341
Females, United States							
Native-born white	13.2	8,851					90,181
Chinese immigrant, 1970–80	12.0	7,391	− 0.16	**	− 0.16	**	2,793
Black immigrant, 1970–80	11.8	7,351	− 0.17	**	− 0.08	*	4,338
Females, Canada							
Native-born white	11.9	7,885					1,454
Chinese immigrant, 1971–81	11.5	7,046	− 0.11	n.s.	− 0.20	n.s.	584
Black immigrant, 1971–81	11.2	6,607	− 0.16	n.s.	− 0.15	n.s.	324

[a] Wage and salary employment earnings including self-employment earnings. Canadian earnings are standardized to 1980 US dollars.

[b] The sample consists of members of the labor force who are aged 16–64; who have earnings over $100; who reside in a Standard Metropolitan Statistical Area (for the United States) or a Census Metropolitan Area (for Canada) with a population over 500,000; and who are either native-born whites or black or Chinese immigrants who have arrived during the ten years preceding the census.

[c] The overall earnings figures for each immigrant group express the proportions by which they differ from the earnings of native-born whites for each country and gender. The significance test for each US group (** denotes $p < 0.001$, * denotes $p < 0.01$) shows the difference between its position and the position of native-born American whites of the same gender. The significance test for each Canadian group (++ denotes $p < 0.001$, + denotes $p < 0.01$) shows the difference between its relative position and the relative position of the same group in the United States.

[d] The net earnings figures are based on a single pooled regression analysis with (unlogged) earnings as dependent, dummy variables for Chinese immigrants, black immigrants, Canada, Chinese immigrants in Canada, and black immigrants in Canada, and with control variables for years of education (quadratic), years of experience (quadratic), knowledge of English (in Quebec, French; in Montreal, English or French), and hours worked. The results are expressed as a proportion of the white native-born earnings for each country and gender. The significance tests are the same as those used in the overall analysis.

Sources: US data are from the 1980 census microdata A file, 5/100; Canadian data are from the 1981 microdata file of individuals, 2/100.

between the relative position of recent black male immigrants in Canada, net of job qualifications, and the relative position of their counterparts in the United States is not statistically significant. The relative position of recent Chinese male immigrants is better in Canada and in this case the difference is statistically significant, though it is not large.[13] None of the cross-national comparisons for racial-minority immigrant women is statistically significant.

Thus, the data show that at least in two important cases racial-minority male immigrants experience more inequality in the United States than they do in Canada. The difference is largely attributable to the fact that black and Chinese male immigrants in the United States have less education relative to native-born white males than do their counterparts in Canada. If allowance is made for the difference in relative levels of education, the difference in earnings becomes small in the case of immigrant Chinese men and statistically insignificant in the cases of black men and black and Chinese women.

Assimilation and Native-Born Descendants of Immigrants

An immigrant's earnings generally increase over time. Chiswick (1986, 184) estimates the number of years it takes various immigrant

---

13 A statistically significant difference is one that is unlikely to have occurred simply by chance. The notes to Table 12 indicate the precise criteria that we have used for statistical significance. The somewhat smaller disadvantage of Chinese immigrant males in Canada is statistically significant in the sense that the observed cross-national difference would be expected to arise by chance only four times in 100 (hence $p = 0.04$). A useful analysis of US and Canadian census data on Chinese males, by Duleep and Regets (1992, 427–431), is consistent with these results. They found that Chinese immigrants in Canada were younger and more proficient in English than their counterparts in the United States, but that this gave the Chinese in Canada only a temporary advantage:

> Our expectations concerning the effect of higher language proficiency on the relative earnings of Canadian immigrants are not borne out. Although Chinese immigrants to the United States initially earn less relative to the Chinese immigrants to Canada, after ten years the relative earnings of the US Chinese immigrants surpass the earnings of their Canadian counterparts. (470.).

groups in the United States to achieve the same earnings as native-born Americans of the same racial background. The initial earnings of immigrants from Europe, adjusted for human capital and demographic characteristics, are about 10 percent less than those of native-born whites. This deficit disappears in approximately 10 to 15 years. For non-European immigrants, whose initial earnings are much lower on average, other things being equal, than those of European immigrants, progress is slower even when it is measured against the position of native-born Americans of the same racial background. Mexican immigrants take 15 to 20 years to achieve the same earnings as native-born Americans of Mexican origin. For Asian groups combined, the time required to achieve the same earnings as native-born Asian-Americans is 15 to 25 years. Borjas (1986, 479), too, shows that it takes non-European immigrants much longer than European immigrants to catch up to native-born Americans of the same racial background. Thus, it is by no means clear that the racial-minority immigrants are moving toward parity with native-born white Americans.

Borjas (1985) argues, however, that it may be a mistake to assume — as Chiswick does — that recent immigrants will progress as rapidly as earlier immigrants did, since the most recent immigrants have less productive capability than earlier immigrants did when they arrived, or at least have characteristics of less appeal to employers. Borjas suggests using data from successive censuses to separate the effect on earnings of declining immigrant productivity from the effect of immigrant progress.

For example, one might measure the progress of immigrants who arrived in the United States during the 1965–69 period by comparing their earnings in the 1970 census with their earnings in the 1980 census.[14] One might then measure changes in the productivity of recent immigrants by comparing the position of the 1965–69 immigrants in the 1970 census with that of the 1975–79 immigrants

---

14 This calculation would ignore changes in the population base as a result of return migration or other factors.

in the 1980 census. Borjas performs this type of analysis for various groups and compares the results with the earnings of the native-born in the corresponding racial groups. He finds that recent immigrants in 1980 were worse off than their counterparts in 1970 and that some of the difference is indeed attributable to a decline in the productivity of recent immigrants during the period. The differences vary somewhat from group to group. They are greater for blacks and Cubans, for example, than they are for whites or Asians. Borjas does not identify any particular cause for differences among groups (Borjas 1985, 480–482; see also Jasso and Rosenzweig 1988). Baker and Benjamin (1992) and Bloom, Grenier, and Gunderson (1991) have conducted comparable analyses for Canada and obtained comparable results.

Lieberson and Waters (1988, ch. 5) examine the earnings of native-born members of racial minorities in the United States. Their analysis identifies individuals on the basis of their reported "ancestry" and distinguishes persons of "black" ancestry, most of whom probably are part of the indigenous black population, from persons of various Asian and Hispanic ancestries and "African, Caribbean, Pacific" ancestry, most of whom are probably descendants of recent immigrants. Lieberson and Waters (1988, 155) emphasize that "the division between whites and non-whites remains strong, even as the division that once existed between whites has largely disappeared." Their findings make it clear, however, that different racial minorities fare differently. After adjustment for education, earnings are lowest for those who report Puerto Rican and black ancestry; higher for native-born Americans of Mexican, South Asian, and "African, Caribbean, Pacific" ancestry; and highest for the native-born of Asian, but not South Asian, origins. Only the last group is not at a disadvantage relative to whites (Lieberson and Waters 1988, 152–153). The somewhat higher standing of some of these groups relative to their immigrant counterparts may imply assimilation to the mainstream standard. One specific finding is of special interest. The earnings disadvantage of native-born Americans of "African, Caribbean, Pacific" ancestry, most of whom are descendants of black immigrants, is about half the earnings disadvantage of native-born Americans of "black" ancestry, most of whom are members of the indigenous black population. Interviews reported by Waters (1991a, 1991b) suggest that second-generation members of the Caribbean community in the United States expect to do better than members of the indigenous American black community. They very often reject identification with American blacks for reasons having to do with work-related values.[15]

Gender and race interact to affect earnings. Variations in earnings by race are smaller among native-born women than they are among native-born men. "The color line is less sharply defined for women than for men" (Lieberson and Waters 1988, 139). In some groups, such as those of Asian origin, the position of women relative to the female benchmark is better than the position of men relative to the male benchmark (ibid.; see also Gwartney and Long 1978; and Carlson and Swartz 1988, especially 538–540). Mexican-American women and men appear to be equally disadvantaged.

Boyd (1992b) uses 1986 Canadian census data in an analysis of the Canadian-born racial-minority population. Her results suggest that native-born racial minorities are less disadvantaged than immigrant members of such minorities. After adjustment for group differences in age, region and Census Metropolitan Area, marital status, education, occupation, and hours and weeks worked, the earnings of non-European immigrant men were 82 percent of the earnings of European immigrant men. The earnings of native-born men of non-European origin were 96 percent of the earnings of native-born men of European origin. The earnings of immigrant women of non- European origin were 90 percent of the earnings of immigrant women of European origin. The earnings of native-born women of non-European origin, after adjustment, were slightly

---

15 The children of black immigrants "set up an opposition in their minds between the culture and values of lower class Black Americans, which includes lack of discipline, poverty, lack of a work ethic, laziness, bad child rearing practices and lack of respect for education and their parents, and ethnic groups values, which include valuing education, strict discipline for children, a strong work ethic and social mobility. They try to impress others that they are Jamaican or Haitian and most definitely *not* American black" (Waters 1991b, 32).

higher than those of native-born women of European-origin. Racial disadvantage in Canada is less for the native-born than it is for immigrants. Christofides and Swidinsky (1994) find similar patterns in their analysis of the 1989 Labour Market Activity Survey.

We have repeated Boyd's analysis to identify the effect of specific racial origins on the earnings of native-born Canadians; our findings appear in Table 13. As in the United States, the earnings of racial minorities vary substantially from group to group. In 1985, black male immigrants earned $7,558 less, or 26 percent less, than male immigrants of European origin. If one takes human capital endowments such as years of education into account, the deficiency was $6,373, or 22 percent. Native-born black males earned $6,584 less, or 24 percent less, than native-born males of European origin. When human capital endowments are taken into account, the deficiency falls to $2,996, or 11 percent. As in the United States, therefore, the earnings disadvantage of native-born black males of mostly Caribbean or other foreign ancestry is less than that of foreign-born black males, though it is still significant. There is a greater decline in disadvantage in the case of the East- and Southeast Asian group. Foreign-born males of East- and Southeast-Asian origin earn 21 percent less than do male immigrants of European origin, net of human capital. The disadvantage is comparable to that of foreign-born blacks. Native-born males of East- and Southeast-Asian origin, however, earn only 6 percent less than comparable native-born males of European origin — a disadvantage somewhat less than the disadvantage measured here for native-born black males. South and West Asians as a group are less disadvantaged than either blacks or East and Southeast Asians. Native-born members of this group do not have a statistically significant disadvantage relative to native-born whites, either before or after one takes account of human capital.

Racial-minority immigrant women are at a disadvantage relative to immigrant women of European origin in Canadian society, but this racial difference becomes statistically insignificant among native-born women. Again, this finding is similar to the Lieberson and Waters findings for the United States.

In summary, data on the earnings of racial-minority immigrants in the two countries suggest that immigrants in Canada are in a better position than immigrants in the United States. This is so, however, primarily because immigrants in Canada have more education relative to the native-born than do immigrants in the United States. The net earnings differentials after adjustment for education and other human capital variables indicate little, if any, difference between the two countries. In particular, black immigrants in both countries seem to earn between 70 and 80 percent of what the benchmark group earns. This figure is comparable to the net earnings disadvantage experienced by native-born African-Americans. Asian immigrants may be similarly disadvantaged, though there is variation among Asian groups, and certain groups, such as South Asians, may be less disadvantaged than blacks are. In both countries, the native-born descendants of immigrants seem to experience less disadvantage than immigrants do.

The Debate over Discrimination and Other Sources of Immigrant Disadvantage

In both Canada and the United States, there is a debate about how to interpret the earnings disadvantages of racial minorities, net of education and other demographic variables. Some analysts attribute these earnings disadvantages to racial discrimination by employers. Others attribute them to unmeasured human-capital deficiencies, such as poor quality of education, or less ambition or "talent." Still others carefully avoid deciding between discrimination and other explanations for minority group disadvantages and simply refer to the inability of these groups to translate education into occupation and income at the same level as the rest of the population.

For the purposes of our cross-national comparison, the question of the extent to which earnings disparities are caused by racial discrimination is an important one. Our general objective is to compare evidence related to ethnic and racial tolerance in Canada and the United States. The issue of racial discrimination is critical to this objective. In Chapter 4, we reviewed evidence that direct discrimi-

Table 13: *The Effects of Racial Origin on the Annual Earnings of the Foreign-Born and Native-Born in Canada, 1985[a]*

Ethnic Origin[b]	Earnings							
	1985 C$	Overall[c]		Net of Human Capital[d]		Net of Human Capital and Occupation[e]		Number in Sample
Males, Foreign-born								
White	29,570							23,856
Black	22,012	− 0.26	***	− 0.22	***	− 0.17	***	738
East and Southeast Asian	23,748	− 0.21	***	− 0.21	***	− 0.17	***	1,858
South and West Asian	26,378	− 0.11	***	− 0.13	***	− 0.12	***	1,469
Multiple and other	22,745	− 0.07	***	− 0.09	***	− 0.07	***	1,649
Males, Canadian-born								
White	26,938							64,426
Aboriginal	17,000	− 0.37	***	− 0.08	***	− 0.10	***	904
Black	20,354	− 0.24	***	− 0.11	*	− 0.08	n.s.	100
East and Southeast Asian	25,722	+ 0.05	n.s.	− 0.06	*	− 0.06	*	282
South and West Asian	21,088	+ 0.22	*	+ 0.10	n.s.	+ 0.10	n.s.	48
Multiple and other	26,016	+ 0.03	***	− 0.01	n.s.	− 0.00	n.s.	10,231
Females, Foreign-born								
White	15,015							10,318
Black	15,695	+ 0.05	n.s.	− 0.04	*	− 0.05	*	832
East and Southeast Asian	15,630	+ 0.04	*	− 0.07	***	− 0.05	***	1,832
South and West Asian	14,068	− 0.06	**	− 0.13	***	− 0.10	***	1,025
Multiple and other	15,802	+ 0.05	**	− 0.02	n.s.	− 0.03	n.s.	1,677
Females, Canadian-born								
White	15,052							51,744
Aboriginal	11,526	− 0.23	***	− 0.02	n.s.	− 0.05	*	643
Black	14,303	− 0.05	n.s.	− 0.06	n.s.	− 0.05	n.s.	90
East and Southeast Asian	19,301	+ 0.28	***	+ 0.05	n.s.	+ 0.04	n.s.	271
South and West Asian	18,105	+ 0.20	n.s.	− 0.05	n.s.	− 0.07	n.s.	47
Multiple and other	15,506	+ 0.03	***	− 0.01	*	− 0.02	*	9,397

Table 13:   *Notes and Source*

[a] The sample consists of persons aged 25–64 who were non-self-employed, wage-earning labor force participants in 1985.

[b] "East and Southeast Asian" includes Chinese, Filipino, and East/Southeast Asian origins. "South and West Asian" includes West Asian and Arab origins and South Asian origins. "Multiple and other" includes other single origin; British and other; French and other; British, French, and other; and other multiple origins.

[c] The overall earnings figures for each immigrant group express the proportions by which they differ from the earnings of native-born whites for each country and gender. In the significance tests, *** denotes $p < 0.001$, ** denotes $p < 0.01$, and * denotes $p < 0.05$.

[d] The human capital variables are education in years, education squared, experience (age minus education minus five years), experience squared, university degree or not, English-speaking or not, bilingual or not, allophone or not, government employee or not, ever married or not, province of residence (Atlantic, Yukon–Northwest Territories, Ontario, Prairies, British Columbia), residence in a city with a population of at least 100,000 or not, weeks worked in 1985, and full-time or part-time employment in 1985.

[e] The available 16 occupational categories were entered into the regression equation as 15 dummy variables: managerial, administrative, and related; natural sciences, engineering, and mathematics; social sciences and related; teaching and related; medicine and health; artistic, literary, recreational, and related; clerical and related; sales; service; farming, horti-cultural, and animal husbandry; other primary; processing; machining and product fabri-cating, assembling, and repairing; construction trades; transport and equipment operating.

Source: 1986 Canadian census microdata file of individuals, 2/100.

natory behavior of employers may be of comparable magnitude in the two countries. However, it is also important to know what effect this discrimination — or other forms of discrimination — may have on the earnings disadvantages of minorities that we have described in this chapter. We will, accordingly, consider the following two questions. First, what is the status of the debate over the relevance of discrimination to minority economic disadvantage? Second, what does the comparison of net earnings disadvantages tell us about the effect of racial discrimination on the economic disadvantages of minorities in the two countries?

Identifying discrimination in labor force data is an uncertain business at best. The main problem is the difficulty in measuring the productivity-value of job-related skills. If discrimination is defined as lower earnings on the basis of race or immigrant status rather than on the basis of poorer productivity-related skills, then one must measure such skills. Yet no one has found a way to measure the productivity-relevance of individual workers' skills in a labor force survey, apart from using the standard variables of years of education work experience, and a few others.[16] Education and experience are not unambiguously related to productivity. There is little or no consensus on which human capital variables are important, or on how they should be measured (see Heckman and Hotz 1986).

Hence the analysis of discrimination in labor force data may either overestimate discrimination or underestimate the actual impact of discrimination (see Reitz 1980b, 157–158). If unmeasured productivity-relevant qualifications are lower in disadvantaged groups, then these unmeasured qualifications — and not discrimination — might cause the earnings disadvantages. Ignoring unmeasured qualifications would lead one to overestimate the impact of direct discrimination. On the other hand, the analysis may underestimate indirect forms of discrimination, if the measured qualifica-

---

16 Sometimes earnings themselves are used, but this approach assumes that employers assign earnings on the basis of productivity and hence begs the whole question of discrimination.

tions are themselves discriminatory, or if there is discriminatory access to qualifications (see Berg 1971; Collins 1979).

In the United States, Borjas (1990, 82) has questioned the relevance of discrimination to the labor market disadvantages of specific groups of immigrants. He says that "the available evidence...does not support the assertion that immigrants are systematically discriminated against" and cites research on Hispanic immigrants by Reimers (1983).[17] Reimers uses the 1976 Survey of Income and Education and shows that, after adjustments for education, work experience, and a number of other individual characteristics, plus an index of local living costs, and after correcting for sample-selection bias,[18] Mexican men earned between 6 and 8 percent less than non-Hispanic white men; Puerto Rican men earned about 18 percent less.

These data on Mexicans and Puerto Ricans do not show an absence of discrimination, for at least three reasons. The first reason, not often recognized, arises from the fact that identifying discrimination by adjusting for the effects of levels of education requires that we know the effects of comparable levels of education in the benchmark group. Because the average levels of education of Mexican immigrants and Puerto Rican migrants are so far below those in the mainstream, the earnings of comparably educated members of the benchmark group cannot be known precisely, so a meaningful adjustment is not really possible.[19] Second, as noted above, Reimers

---

17 See also Reimers 1985, 27–75; Abowd and Killingsworth 1985, 77–125; and Bean and Tienda 1987.

18 Discrimination refers to group differences in wage offers, which in the case of the Mexicans (and other disadvantaged groups) are underestimated because those who receive the lowest offers are likely to leave the labor market altogether. This selection bias was taken into account using the procedure developed by Heckman (1979).

19 We alluded to this problem in footnote 9, above. The analysis of discrimination based on statistical regression actually compares Mexican or Puerto Rican earnings with the downward extrapolation of patterns established within a comparatively much better educated native-born group. The comparisons are inevitably artificial. What earnings might actually be observed among native-born persons whose education is comparable to levels of education typical of Mexican immigrants is anyone's guess.

does in fact find substantial earnings disadvantages net of adjust-ments, a result that points to the existence of some degree of direct discrimination. Third, the net earnings disadvantages for Mexicans and Puerto Ricans may ignore significant indirect discrimination; that is, the low levels of education of the Mexican- or Puerto Rican-born migrants may underestimate the actual productive value of their work. Bonacich (1989–90), in a qualitative study of Mexican-American experience in Los Angeles, shows that formal education is not a foolproof guide to the productive value of work performed by Mexican immigrants in many types of factory jobs.[20] These issues are unlikely to be resolved in labor force data. We might add that if discrimination reduces work experience, its effects are compounded.

The possibility of discrimination against other groups in the United States, such as black or Asian immigrants, is of greater significance to the comparison with Canada, where there are also significant populations of such immigrants. In regard to immigrants in general, Borjas (1990, 82) states that "there is no evidence suggest-ing that immigrant labor is cheaper than equally skilled native labor." Presumably such a statement is based on the possibility that, for groups with substantial earnings disadvantages net of formal education or language skills — particularly black immigrants, but also certain Asian groups — lower unmeasured skills may explain the lower net earnings. Some researchers have attempted to measure additional productivity-relevant characteristics, in order to refine the analysis and thus better address the issue of discrimination.[21] Their results have not however disproved the discrimination hypothesis.

One issue concerns foreign education and experience. An im-migrant with the same number of years of education or work expe-rience as a native might earn less because his education and experience

---

20 Borjas has a different view: "It is difficult to take seriously the conjecture that the typical Mexican illegal alien is perfectly interchangeable with the typical native in the labor force, or even with an unskilled young black residing in Watts or Harlem" (Borjas 1990, 82).

21 Stolzenberg (1975) suggests that there are some ways in which labor force survey data can demonstrate the importance of discrimination.

abroad are not relevant to job productivity under US or Canadian conditions. In a useful pair of studies, Treiman et al. (1986–87) and Treiman and Lee (1988) examine occupational status and earnings, respectively, among men in 28 ethnic groups in Los Angeles.[22] They distinguish empirically between education and experience acquired abroad and education and experience acquired in the United States, and find that, in the Los Angeles labor market, foreign experience does indeed have less value than US experience.

These findings could reflect indirect discrimination against foreign credentials. When foreign education or experience is found to "explain" low occupational status or earnings, it may be that the research is simply measuring the negative perceptions that employers have of foreign education and experience. If the negative perceptions are correct — that is, if foreign education is in fact less valuable in production — then low pay is in a sense justified. If they are not correct, then low pay is discriminatory. Discrimination based on requirements for "domestic experience" that are not justified by productivity-relevance is frequently raised as an issue in both Canada and the United States. The issue has been officially recognized in Australia (see Australia 1982; Iredale 1988). Formal barriers in skilled trades and professions block immigrant advancement. Denigration of foreign qualifications, when it cannot be justified by job requirements, is an example of indirect discrimination — the use of discriminatory criteria for hiring or promotion.

The Los Angeles studies found that, even after adjustments for foreign education and experience, significant disadvantages remained for many groups, particularly in earnings. Most ethnic variations in occupational status were explained by adjustments for years of schooling, where education was completed, years of foreign experience, years of domestic experience, competence in English, and period of immigration. Only for Cubans, Mexicans, and South Americans was discrimination a "real possibility" (Treiman et al.

---

22 The survey included five counties (Los Angeles, Orange, Riverside, San Bernardino, and Ventura) with a total population of 12 million.

1986–87, 22). By contrast, the earnings analysis showed that males in all non-European groups earned less than expected, even after adjustments for a list of individual attributes even longer than the one used in the analysis of status.[23] The authors offer this assessment of their findings:

> Seldom are results so clear cut. Given the enormous diversity in the socioeconomic background, historical position, and culture of the 28 ethnic groups distinguished here, an inference that some sort of "discrimination" against "non-white" groups is operative is hard to resist. But just what the mechanisms of discrimination are is by no means clear. (Treiman and Lee 1988, 21.)

After adjustment, Asians earned 95 percent of the overall mean, Hispanics 93 percent, and blacks 80 percent. "An inference of continuing and substantial discrimination against blacks seems difficult to avoid" (Treiman and Lee 1988, 22–23).

Cultural variations among racial minority groups could explain some of their residual earnings disadvantages. It may be either that racial discrimination is intensified by cultural markers or that variations in worker productivity are related to culture. Some form of cultural or educational assimilation may explain why the native-born descendants of racial-minority immigrants appear to experience less net disadvantage, and perhaps less direct discrimination, than racial-minority immigrants. We have, however, found no research that explores these issues systematically.

In the United States, then, direct racial discrimination remains a possible or even likely cause of at least some earnings disadvantages of immigrants and racial minorities. This direct discrimination may vary in its impact on specific groups and appears to be less for the first native-born generation. Indirect discrimination may also be significant, not only for Mexicans and Puerto Ricans, but also for

---

23 The new list adds to the old occupational status; sector of employment (federal state, or local government or other); industry; whether self-employed, unpaid family worker, employee of own corporation, or employed; whether drives own motor vehicle to work (in Los Angeles probably as much an indicator of income as a determinant); marital status; veteran status; and disability status.

many immigrant groups whose educational levels are higher but still not on a par with those of native-born white Americans.

In Canada, the Economic Council of Canada report on immigrants (Swan et al. 1991, 93) also questions the importance of racial discrimination in affecting the earnings of immigrants. It states that "there is no significant discrimination against...coloured immigrants." This conclusion is based on a study of 1986 census data by de Silva (1992), which attempts to show that the educational and cultural attributes of immigrants, rather than discrimination, are the cause of their low earnings. The Economic Council study tries to show this by examining net earnings disadvantages among racial minority immigrants who had grown up in Canada and whose divergence from the educational and cultural mainstream would therefore be less than that of adult immigrants. If racial minority immigrants who arrived in Canada in early childhood suffer no disadvantages, then the existence of racial discrimination is disproved.

The Economic Council's analysis is seriously flawed, however, by several statistical and measurement problems (see Reitz 1993; 1994). For one thing, it is based on country of birth categories rather than on ethnic and racial origins.[24] What is more important, the numbers of cases are very small for most of the country-of-origin groups considered.[25] Finally, the analysis combines women and

---

24 The African country-of-birth categories in particular are not good indicators of racial or ethnic origins. Not all members of these categories are members of racial minorities, a fact that one can confirm by cross-classifying birth place with ethnic origin, using the same 2 percent 1986 census sample. Of immigrants to Canada born in North Africa, for example, about half were South Asian by ethnic origin and most of the rest were of European ethnic origin; virtually none was black. Of immigrants in the category "other Africa," 15 percent were black, 12 percent were European, and 52 percent were South Asian by ethnic origin. The Asian and Caribbean country-of-birth categories, by contrast, did contain a preponderance of persons of the expected racial or ethnic origins.

25 In only two instances — Caribbean and East Asian — is the analysis of country-of-origin categories based on more than 30 cases. The data for these groups show significant disadvantage (see text below). In other instances, the statistical base is extremely weak. The Council report does not mention the smallness of the samples, but one can estimare their size by applying the percentage distributions in Table 7 (de Silva 1992, 29) to the sample sizes reported in Table 8 (ibid., 30). We...

men, using gender only as a control variable. The evidence is not in fact sufficient to support the Economic Council's conclusion that "the evidence goes against the view that there is systematic earnings discrimination against immigrants on the basis of colour."

The most reliable data are those for the largest racial minorities — namely, blacks and East Asian (mostly Chinese) immigrants. They show consistent and substantial net earnings disadvantages for both adult immigrants and immigrants raised in Canada. It is not surprising that racial discrimination should fall more heavily on some racial-minority groups, or on some ethnic groups within racial categories, than it falls on others. As in the United States, culture may reinforce racial distinctions — that is, members of the majority group may assign a greater negative value to some racial minority cultures than to others. Discrimination against some Asian groups may be more intense than discrimination against others; discrimination against Caribbean-born blacks may be more intense than discrimination against their Canadian-born descendants.

In Canada, then, as in the United States, significant earnings disadvantages remain for black and certain Asian immigrants even after adjustments are made for a wide variety of individual attributes that are potentially relevant to the productive value of work. Since there is, as we showed in Chapter 4, persuasive evidence of racial discrimination in employment in both Canada and the United States, and since labor force analysis, despite its limitations, does raise at least the serious possibility that discrimination accounts for part of the earnings disadvantages of racial-minority immigrants in the two countries, it is reasonable to infer that racial discrimination may indeed account in part, in both countries, for these disadvantages.

The similarity of patterns of immigrant earnings net of education and other demographic characteristics in the two countries does

---

Note 25 - cont'd.

...have confirmed the smallness of the numbers in a replication. For persons born in Southeast Asia, for example, the number of cases, male and female, was only 10. For "other Africa" it was 13, for North Africa it was 17, for West Asia it was 27, and for South Asia it was 30.

not support the hypothesis that direct discrimination has less impact in Canada than in the United States. All analysts agree that the more discrimination there is against a group, the greater the net earnings disadvantage for that group will be. If discrimination is an important cause of racial disadvantage, whether in Canada or in the United States, then one would expect it to increase the earnings disadvantages of immigrant groups, net of education and other demographics. If discrimination were a more serious problem in the United States than it is in Canada, then one would expect immigrant earnings net of education to be lower for racial minority groups in the United States. Yet this is not the case. Therefore, the hypothesis that there is less discrimination in Canada is not supported. In this respect, the process of incorporation does not appear to be drastically different in the two countries, or even significantly different.

The largest difference between the two countries may be in the potential for indirect discrimination that arises from credentialism. For many immigrant groups, the overall earnings gap is larger in the United States; this is so mainly because the immigrant education-gap is larger there as well. To the extent that education may be overused as a job qualification in both the United States and Canada, earnings disadvantages based on lower immigrant education levels may constitute a form of indirect discrimination. Discrimination of this type would be greater in the United States.

Summary

Racial-minority immigrants in the United States earn less on average, relative to the native-born population, than do their counterparts in Canada. This is so largely because they have less education relative to the native-born. If one takes this and other differences in human capital into account, there appears to be little, if any, difference between the earnings of racial-minority immigrants in each of the two countries. Largely because of the difference in education, the economic incorporation of immigrant racial minorities probably takes longer in the United States than it does in Canada. The capacity of racial-minority immigrants to turn human capital into earnings is similar in the two countries.

The extent to which discrimination against minorities and immigrants may be a cause of their lower earnings is controversial. Some researchers in both countries argue that the earnings disadvantages of immigrants that remain after adjustments for measurable job qualifications — such as education, language knowledge, and work experience — are attributable to discrimination. Others argue that they are a result of other human capital deficiencies of racial minorities. We have shown that analysis of this issue has not eliminated discrimination as a possible cause of the lower earnings of racial minority immigrants in either country. The data suggest that the situations are not strikingly different in the two countries. They are not consistent with what one would expect if there were more racial discrimination in employment in the United States than there is in Canada.

The relatively better education of immigrants to Canada supports Porter's (1965) view that Canada relies on immigration for skilled workers more than the United States does. On the other hand, the evidence does not support his view that minority groups in the United States enjoy a reasonable degree of mobility, whereas minority groups in Canada are locked into their entrance status — the "vertical mosaic." Again, the evidence suggests that the processes of mobility in the two countries are similar.

Chapter 6

Conclusions

Our comparison of the Canadian mosaic and the American melting pot reveals that the differences between them are not overwhelming. At any rate, they do not appear to be large enough to justify the distinction implied by the choice of metaphors. When one looks at relations in the two countries between the dominant ethnic groups and ethnic groups composed of immigrants and their descendants, the similarities far outweigh the differences. The differences appear to be limited to specific aspects of relations among ethnic groups in the two countries, and these differences do not add up to major differences between them in the overall pattern of relations. Furthermore, where there are differences, they are much more likely to characterize the attitudes of the majority group toward minorities rather than either their behavior or the experiences of the minorities themselves. The differences between rates of assimilation of minorities in the two countries seem to be small, and the differences vary with the aspect of assimilation considered. Differences in the extent of economic opportunity are small as well.

The first part of our analysis examined attitudes toward the retention of ethnic culture by immigrants and their descendants. Here the findings contradicted the mosaic/melting pot formula: Americans favor cultural retention more than Canadians do. This surprising result emerged from a 1989 Decima survey of opinion in both countries, and we have examined the issue further. We have found that, among Canadians, support for cultural retention has not changed significantly since the introduction of "multiculturalism" as public policy in the early 1970s. This result tells against Lipset's "backlash" hypothesis, as does the fact that ethnic-minority respondents are about as likely as those in the majority (except the French) to support the view that people who come to Canada should try to be more like "us." Finally, residents of cities with the largest numbers of recent immigrants are not more likely than other Canadians to oppose cultural retention.

One factor that does clearly account for at least a small part of the cross-national difference in support for cultural retention by minorities is the higher level of education of the US population. Better-educated, and younger, people tend to favor the idea of cultural retention. More interesting are the differences between Canadians and Americans in the symbolic and political values they assign to the idea. Cultural diversity evokes different feelings in the two countries. In the United States, we found, support for cultural retention is linked to the ideal of individualism, an ideal that has more value for Americans than it does for Canadians. We also found that black Americans more often favor cultural retention than white Americans do, perhaps because they identify to some extent with other groups that they see as being denied the opportunity to participate fully in the US cultural mainstream. It may be that the assertion of minority cultures in the United States is in some respects an anti-establishment or anti-authority viewpoint, reflecting a perception that the dominant ideology is in fact assimilationist. If so, this anti-authority view is fairly widespread across the country.

The issue looks quite different in Canada. In Canada, there is no link between support for cultural retention and support for the ideal of individualism, which, in any case, is less potent in Canada than it is in the United States. And whereas in the United States the largest minority group is inclined to favor the encouragement of cultural retention by immigrants, most members of Canada's principal cultural minority, French-Canadians, strongly oppose immigrant cultural retention. Moreover, contrary to the trend among younger people in other groups across North America, the trend among younger French-Canadians is away from support for cultural retention. French-Canadians are more likely than other Canadians to oppose cultural retention — and its official expression, multiculturalism —

probably because they are concerned about the possible threat to their own group position within Canada, which they perceive as precarious. If black Americans see immigrant ethnic groups as allies, French-Canadians may see them as competitors.

Support for immigrant cultural retention in Canada appears to reflect an establishment perspective rather than an oppositional one. Contrary to expectation, we found that support for cultural retention in Canada (and to a lesser extent in the United States as well) is greater in the British-origin group than it is in any other European-origin group. Relatively well-educated persons of British origin constitute the only population group in which support for immigrant cultural retention is higher in Canada than it is in the United States. Some of our data suggest that support for cultural retention is identified with those who strongly assert Canadian national distinctiveness or independence. By contrast, the "backlash" in Canada against the idea of cultural retention may come primarily from members of ethnic minorities of European origin who — not unlike French-Canadians — are worried that cultural pluralism will lead to their marginalization in Canada. This is a hypothesis, one that we cannot explore without trend data on population subgroups.

We should emphasize, however, that support for multiculturalism is not necessarily the same as support for the actual encouragement of minority cultural retention. In Canada, we found, most people think of multiculturalism in terms of acceptance rather than encouragement. Attitudes toward cultural retention are not necessarily the same as attitudes toward multiculturalism in the United States either. In the United States, of course, the term multiculturalism is not connected with any government policies. Some Americans see multiculturalism as not only anti-authority, but also as a threat to national unity, and as anti-individualistic. For example, a recent bestseller by the historian Arthur M. Schlesinger, Jr., *The Disuniting of America: Reflections on a Multicultural Society* (1992), attacks what he calls multiculturalism as part of a reformist, "politically correct" assault on the traditional American values, including not only assimilation and the melting pot, but also the traditional "Eurocentric" curriculum. He links multiculturalism with various claims that minorities, women, and other disadvantaged groups are making for compensatory treatment. Because multiculturalism makes claims based on group membership, it is opposed to the value of individual identity and individualism:

> Instead of a nation composed of individuals making their own unhampered choices, America increasingly sees itself as composed of groups more or less ineradicable in their ethnic character. The multiethnic dogma abandons historic purposes, replacing assimilation by fragmentation, integration by separatism. It belittles *unum* and glorifies *pluribus*. (Schlesinger 1992, 16–17.)

Schlesinger cites Canada as an example of a country in which cultural pluralism undermines national unity.

Schlesinger's discussion of multiculturalism in the United States does not reflect public attitudes toward immigrant cultural retention. Americans today tend to see minority cultural retention as a contemporary reflection of individualism, not as a threat to it. This point emerged in our analysis of US survey data, and it is also reflected in popular commentaries.[1] Most Americans who favor a society that encourages immigrants to retain their traditional cultures favor it not because they are hostile to individualism but because they support it. In fact, as we have noted, American individualism seems to be one of the factors that has produced broader public support for immigrant cultural retention in the United States than in Canada.

These cross-national differences are differences in attitude, and attitudes may or may not be related to behavior. It is conceivable that, although Americans express a more favorable view of cultural retention than Canadians do, their behavior is quite the other way; the

---

1 A black American columnist, Robert L. Steinback, wrote in the *Miami Herald* (August 17, 1993, 1B) that "the melting pot is contrary to the American ideal" of individual liberty, because it forces conformity to the white cultural standard. "White Americans who insist on promoting a 'melting pot' that would force compromises in individual identity are actually inhibiting the normal socialization of many young black Americans."

mosaic/melting pot distinction may be justified after all. When we examined *actual* cultural retention, however, as indicated both by subjective measures of ethnic identification and by behavioral measures such as ethnic intermarriage, we found no systematic difference between the two countries. Cultural retention is studied far more intensively in Canada, where the issue has stimulated not only academic interest but government funding — not necessarily in that order — but there are comparable US data for certain key indicators. And the data do not show any consistent differences between rates of assimilation in Canada and the United States. In this respect, there is no difference between the mosaic and the melting pot. Ethnocultural communities are a more visible feature of the social fabric in Canadian cities, particularly Toronto, Montreal, and Vancouver, than they are in most US cities, but the data suggest that this difference is almost entirely a result of the high level of immigration in Canada in recent years.

Our examination of data on the second major issue — discrimination and inequality — also produced some evidence of cross-national differences, but again the differences had more to do with the expressed attitudes of the dominant population than with its behavior. We found no significant differences between the two countries in matters such as the occupational mobility of minorities. In the United States, most of the research relevant to discrimination and inequality has addressed racial prejudice. In Canada, until recently, the issue of equality has arisen primarily in connection with the question of the impact of cultural retention. There is now a small amount of research on race available for Canada, however, so there are some comparable data for key indicators.

The data show that very large majorities in both countries reject racism as an explicit ideology. In both countries as well, the expression of negative racial attitudes has declined markedly over time. Subtle negative racial attitudes persist in the United States; for example, many Americans feel that members of racial minorities are themselves to blame for the disadvantages they suffer. However, survey data show that this view is widespread in Canada, too.

The issue of anti-Semitism, unlike the issue of racial equality has the advantage for our purposes that it presents itself in similar ways in the two countries. By most measures, the minorities of Canadians and Americans that express anti-Semitic attitudes are of similar size — a finding consistent with our findings for attitudes toward racial minorities. Anti-Semitic behavior, too, would appear to be of comparable significance in the two countries.

The most significant cross-national differences appear in measures of the "social distance" of racial minorities. Social distance is a measure of the desire to exclude members of minorities, to keep them at a distance, as reflected in attitudes toward their acceptability as citizens, residents in the same neighborhood, co-workers, and family members. Social-distance measures disclose many similar patterns in Canada and the United States, but there are also some significant differences. The important similarities are three. First, the rank-order in which the dominant group places the minority groups is the same in both countries: north Europeans at the top, south Europeans lower down, and non-Europeans — Asians and blacks — at the bottom. Second, social distances have declined dramatically in both countries over the past few decades. Social distances from minorities measured in certain populations, such as students, are quite comparable in the two countries. Third, while Canadians in recent times have perhaps been more open to immigration than have Americans, and while Canada recently has seen even larger proportional increases in racial-minority populations as a result of immigration than has the United States, in both countries there is now a sharp reduction in support for immigration. Race has emerged as an immigration issue in both countries.

The important differences refer to other particular components of the social-distance scale. Canadians are less likely than Americans to say they would move if a black person moved in next door, and they are less likely to object to interracial marriage. They are not, however, significantly more — or less — willing to accept racial minorities in social clubs. These differences in attitude may arise from specific cross-national differences that are not directly related to racial prejudice. For example, Canadians' more positive attitude toward intermarriage may reflect religious differences between the two countries. Americans' less favorable attitude toward having members of racial minorities as neighbors may be related to the fact that racial minorities there tend to be concentrated in "inner city" slums.

These are all attitude data. The measurement of actual racial discrimination is more difficult. One interesting source of data is employment "field trials." The field trials that have been conducted in the two countries have been fairly small, but they do not suggest any systematic difference between the two in the extent of actual employment discrimination.

We also examined attitudes toward government policies against racial discrimination. A considerable body of US research suggests that Americans oppose government intervention to assist blacks. In Canada, the only relevant survey showed that most Canadians are willing to have government intervene in order to guarantee equal opportunity "for all Canadians," but the question did not mention race. In terms of actual government actions, of course, Americans have placed higher priority than have Canadians on reducing racial discrimination. This is understandable: the larger size of racial minorities in the United States is bound to make racial discrimination a more substantial political issue there. But the fact that Americans assign greater priority to discrimination does not necessarily mean that they have a greater awareness of discrimination or a stronger predisposition in favor of government intervention.

These differences in private attitudes and public actions do not appear to have produced any major cross-national differences in the rate of economic incorporation of immigrant ethnic and racial minorities. People of European origin, whether they are in Canada or the United States, achieve occupational status and earnings roughly commensurate with their levels of education. Immigrants of European origin in Canada are more likely to be recent immigrants and less likely to be well-educated than their counterparts in the United States, and for this reason they have lower occupational status and earnings. But the data suggest that, given Canadian education in the second generation, these people, like their American counterparts, will achieve parity with the dominant groups.

For racial-minority immigrants in both countries, economic incorporation is far slower. There does not appear to be any significant difference in status between black immigrants in each of the two countries in this regard. We reviewed studies of incorporation by others and also prepared our own analysis of the incorporation of specific immigrant groups. The results are fairly clear. Most immigrant groups, including blacks and Chinese, have relatively higher occupational standing in Canada than they do in the United States, but this is so because the education gap between immigrants and the native-born is smaller in Canada, rather than because the two countries treat members of racial minorities with comparable levels of education differently. When adjustments are made for education and work experience, Asian immigrants in both countries earn less than either immigrants of European origin or the native-born, and black immigrants earn less than Asians.

Our findings about employment discrimination against racial minorities do not support the view that there is less racial discrimination in Canada than there is in the United States. The analysis of discrimination is difficult, and although the data clearly indicate that discrimination is significant in both countries, its importance in producing earnings inequalities among racial groups is debatable. The important point for our purposes here is that analyses of comparable data do not show a significant difference between the patterns of discrimination in employment in the two countries. The data do suggest that the historical differences in race relations in the two countries may have produced some differences in racial attitudes; they do not, however, suggest the existence of major differences in the most important area: the predisposition to discriminate against racial minorities. As in the analysis of cultural retention, the differences seem to refer primarily to the attitudes of the dominant groups, not to their behavior or the behavior of the minorities themselves.

Our conclusions are based on the currently available evidence. Not all of the data are as complete as we would like them to be. There are several areas in which more detailed cross-national comparisons would be very useful. Additional research is needed — both research that would compare the economic position of racial-minority immigrants in Canada with that of racial-minority immigrants in the United States and research that would show the formation of ethnocultural communities among immigrants from all groups in both countries.[2]

The general cultural differences between Canada and the United States imply differences of tone in ethnic and race relations in the two countries. The Canadian style is more low-key than the American; moreover, Canadians have a conscious tradition of "tolerance" that Americans do not have. In terms of their effects on the experiences of minority groups, however, these differences are more apparent than real. Some have argued that the Canadian style serves to camouflage underlying racial animosities. We have no data that directly supports this argument, but we can say that the cultural differences between the two countries have not produced less pressure toward conformity in Canada, or less propensity to discriminate in employment or housing.

---

2 One might also compare minority representation among elected officials. Harris and Wilkins (1988) report that the number of black elected officials in the United States increased from 200 in 1965 to 6,500 in 1986. A comparison with developments in Canada (see Megyery 1991), taking account of demographic differences, would be worth making.

References

Abowd, John M., and Makr R. Killingsworth. 1985. "Employment, Wages, and Earnings of Hispanics in the Federal and Nonfederal Sectors: Methodological Issues and Their Empirical Consequences." In *Hispanics in the U.S. Economy*, edited by George Borjas and Marta Tienda, 77–125. Orlando, Fla.: Academic Press.

Adachi, Ken. [1976] 1991. *The Enemy That Never Was: A History of the Japanese Canadians*. Reprint. Toronto: McClelland and Stewart.

Adams, Roy J. 1989. "North American Industrial Relations: Divergent Trends in Canada and the United States." *International Labour Review* 128, 1: 47–64.

Alba, Richard D. 1990. *Ethnic Identity: The Transformation of White America*. New Haven: Yale University Press.

————, and Mitchell B. Chamlin. 1983. "A Preliminary Examination of Ethnic Identification Among Whites." *American Sociological Review* 48: 240–247.

Allen, Walter R., and Reynolds Farley. 1986. "The Shifting Social and Economic Tides of Black America, 1950-1980." *Annual Review of Sociology* 12: 277–306.

Allport, Gordon W. 1954. *The Nature of Prejudice*. Cambridge, Mass.: Addison-Wesley Publishing Co.

Angus Reid Group Inc. 1989. *Immigration to Canada: Aspects of Public Opinion*. Report prepared for Employment and Immigration Canada. Winnipeg: Angus Reid Group Inc.

————. 1991. *Multiculturalism and Canadians: Attitude Study 1991* (National Survey Report). Report submitted to Multiculturalism and Citizenship Canada.

Anti-Defamation League of B'nai Brith. 1991. *1991 Audit of Anti-Semitic Incidents*. New York: Anti-Defamation League of B'nai Brith.

Arnold, Stephen J., and Douglas J. Tigert. 1974. "Canadians and Americans: A Comparative Analysis." *International Journal of Comparative Sociology* 15, 1-2: 68–83.

Australia. 1982. Committee of Inquiry into Recognition of Overseas Qualifications [Fry Committee]. *The Recognition of Overseas Qualifications in Australia*. 2 vols. Canberra: Australian Government Publishing Service.

Badets, Jane. 1993. "Canada's Immigrants: Recent Trends." *Canadian Social Trends* (Summer): 8–11.

Baer, Douglas, Edward Grabb, and William A. Johnston. 1990. "The Values of Canadians and Americans: A Critical Analysis and Reassessment." *Social Forces* 68, 3: 693–713.

Baker, Michael, and Dwayne Benjamin. 1992. "The Performance of Immigrants in the Canadian Labour Market." Department of Economics, University of Toronto. Unpublished manuscript.

Barrett, Stanley R. 1987. *Is God a Racist? The Right Wing in Canada*. Toronto: University of Toronto Press.

Basavarajappa, K.G., and Ravi B.P. Verma. 1985. "Asian Immigrants in Canada: Some Findings from 1981 Census." *International Migration* 23, 1 (March): 97–121.

Bean, Frank D., and Marta Tienda. 1987. *The Hispanic Population of the United States*. New York: The Russell Sage Foundation.

Beaujot, Roderic, K.G. Basavarajappa, and R.B.P. Verma. 1988. *Income of Immigrants in Canada: A Census Data Analysis*. Current Demographic Analysis, Statistics Canada Catalogue No. 91-527E. Ottawa: Supply and Services.

Becker, Gary. 1964. *Human Capital*. New York: National Bureau of Economic Research.

———. 1971. *A Theory of Discrimination*, 2d ed. Chicago: University of Chicago Press.

Bell, Daniel. 1973. *The Coming of Post-Industrial Society*. New York: Basic Books.

Berg, Ivar. 1971. *Education and Jobs: The Great Training Robbery*. Boston: Beacon.

Berry, John W., R. Kalin, and D.M. Taylor. 1977. *Multiculturalism and Ethnic Attitudes in Canada*. Ottawa: Supply and Services Canada.

Bibby, Reginald W. 1990. *Mosaic Madness: The Poverty and Potential of Life in Canada*. Toronto: Stoddart.

Blau, Francine D., and Andrea H. Beller. 1988. "Trends in Earnings Differentials by Gender." *Industrial and Labor Relations Review* 41: 513–529.

Blau, Peter M., Terry C. Blum, and Joseph E. Schwartz. 1982. "Heterogeneity and Intermarriage." *American Sociological Review* 47: 45–62.

Bloom, David, Gilles Grenier, and Morley Gunderson. 1991. "Has the Canadian Labour Market Lost Its Ability to Assimilate Immigrants?" Unpublished manuscript.

B'nai Brith Canada. 1991. *The Review of Anti-Semitism in Canada*. Ontario: The League for Human Rights of B'nai Brith Canada.

Bobo, Lawrence. 1987. "Racial Attitudes and the Status of Black Americans: A Social Psychological View of Change since the 1940s." Paper prepared for the Committee on the Status of Black Americans, National Research Council, Washington, DC.

———. 1988. "Group Conflict, Prejudice, and the Paradox of Contemporary Racial Attitudes." In *Eliminating Racism: Means and Controversies*, edited by Phyllis A. Katz and Dalmas A. Taylor, 85–114. New York: Plenum.

Bogardus, Emory S. 1958. "Racial Distance Changes in the United States During the Past Thirty Years." *Sociology and Social Research* 43: 127–135.

———. 1967. *A Forty-Year Racial Distance Study*. Los Angeles: University of Southern California Press.

Bonacich, Edna. 1972. "A Theory of Ethnic Antagonism: The Split Labor Market." *American Sociological Review* 37, 5 (October): 547-559.

———. 1989–90. "Asian and Latina Immigrants in the Los Angeles Garment Industry: An Exploration of the Relationship between Capitalism and Racial Oppression." Los Angeles: University of California, Institute for Social Science Research, Working Papers in the Social Sciences, vol. 5, no. 13.

Borjas, George J. 1985. "Assimilation, Changes in Cohort Quality, and the Earnings of Immigrants." *Journal of Labor Economics* 3, 4: 463–489.

———. 1986. "The Self-Employment Experience of Immigrants." *The Journal of Human Resources* 21, 4: 485–506.

———. 1988. *International Differences in the Labor Market Performance of Immigrants*. Kalamazoo, Michigan: W.E. Upjohn Institute for Employment Research.

———. 1990. *Friends or Strangers: The Impact of Immigrants on the US Economy*. New York: Basic Books.

Boyd, Monica. 1976. "Immigration Policies and Trends: A Comparison of Canada and the United States." *Demography* 13, 1: 83–104.

———. 1986. "Immigrant Women in Canada." In *International Migration: The Female Experience*, edited by R.J. Simon and C.B. Brittell, 45–61. Totowa, NJ: Rowman and Allan Held.

———. 1992a. "Gender Issues in Immigration and Language Fluency." In *Immigration, Language and Ethnicity: Canada and the United States*, edited by Barry R. Chiswick, 305–372. Washington, DC: AEI Press.

———. 1992b. "Gender, Visible Minority and Immigrant Earnings Inequality: Reassessing an Employment Equity Premise." In *Deconstructing a Nation: Immigration, Multiculturalism and Racism in the 1990s Canada*, edited by Vic Satzewich, 279–321. Toronto: Garamond Press.

Boyd, Monica, et al. 1982. "Status Attainment in Canada: Findings of the Canadian Mobility Study." *Canadian Review of Sociology and Anthropology* 18: 657–673.

Breton, Raymond. 1978. "Stratification and Conflict between Ethnolinguistic Communities with Different Social Structures." *Canadian Review of Sociology and Anthropology* 15: 148–157.

———. 1988. "French-English Relations." In *Understanding Canadian Society*, edited by J. Curtis and L. Tepperman, 559–85. Toronto: McGraw Hill-Ryerson.

———. 1992. *Why Meech Failed: Lessons for Canadian Constitutionmaking*. Toronto: C.D. Howe Institute.

———, et al. 1990. *Ethnic Identity and Inequality: Varieties of Experience in a Canadian City*. Toronto: University of Toronto Press.

———, Jeffrey G. Reitz, and Victor F. Valentine. 1980. *Cultural Boundaries and the Cohesion of Canada*. Montreal: Institute for Research on Public Policy.

Briggs, Vernon M., Jr. 1984. *Immigration Policy and the American Labor Force*. Baltimore: Johns Hopkins University Press.

Brotz, Howard. 1981. "Multiculturalism in Canada: A Muddle." *Canadian Public Policy* 6: 41–46.

Bruce, Peter G. 1989. "Political Parties and Labor Legislation in Canada and the U.S." *Industrial Relations* 28, 2: 115–41.

Canadian Human Rights Commission. 1986. *Colloquium on Research on Racial Discrimination*. Ottawa: Canadian Human Rights Commission.

Carlson, Leonard A., and Caroline Swartz. 1988. "The Earnings of Women and Ethnic Minorities, 1959–1979." *Industrial and Labor Relations Review* 41, 4: 530–546.

Castles, Stephen. 1989. *Migrant Workers and the Transformation of Western Societies*. Ithaca, NY, Cornell University, Centre for International Studies, Western Societies Program, Occasional Paper 22.

Center for Applied Research in the Apostolate. 1983. *Values Study of Canada*. Washington, DC: The Center.

Chiswick, Barry R. 1978. "The Effect of Americanization on the Earnings of Foreign-Born Men." *Journal of Political Economy* 86, 5: 897–921.

———. 1986. "Is the New Immigration Less Skilled Than the Old?" *Journal of Labor Economics* 4, 2: 168–192.

———. 1988. "Immigration Policy, Source Countries, and Immigrant Skills: Australia, Canada, and the United States." In *The Economics of Immigration: Proceedings of a Conference at the Australian National University, 22–23 April, 1987*, edited by Lyle Baker and Paul Miller. Canberra: Australian Government Publishing Service.

Christofides, L.N., and R. Swidinsky. 1994. "Wage Determination by Gender and Visible Minority Status: Evidence from the 1989 LMAS." *Canadian Public Policy* 22, 1: 34–51.

Clark, S.D. [1950] 1962. *The Developing Canadian Community*. Reprint. Toronto: University of Toronto Press.

Collins, Randall. 1979. *The Credential Society: An Historical Sociology of Education and Stratification*. New York: Academic Press.

Collins, Sharon. 1983. "The Making of the Black Middle Class." *Social Problems* 30: 369–82.

Cooney, Rosemary Santana, and Vilma Ortiz. 1983. "Nativity, National Origin, and Hispanic Female Participation in the Labor Force." *Social Science Quarterly* 64: 510–523.

Crawford, Craig, and James Curtis. 1979. "English Canadian-American Differences in Value Orientations." *Studies in Comparative International Development* 14: 23–44.

Cuneo, Carl J., and James E. Curtis. 1975. "Social Ascription in the Educational and Occupational Status of Urban Canadians." *Canadian Review of Sociology and Anthropology* 12, 1: 6–24.

Darroch, A.G. 1979. "Another Look at Ethnicity, Stratification, and Social Mobility in Canada." *Canadian Journal of Sociology* 4, 1: 1–25.

Davis, Morris, and Joseph F. Krauter. 1971. *The Other Canadians: Profiles of Six Minorities*. Toronto: Methuen.

de Silva, Arnold. 1992. *Earnings of Immigrants: A Comparative Analysis*. Ottawa: Economic Council of Canada.

Dion, Kenneth L. 1985. "Social Distance Norms in Canada: Effects of Stimulus Characteristics and Dogmatism." *International Journal of Psychology* 20: 743–749.

Driedger, Leo, and Richard Mezoff. 1981. "Ethnic Prejudice and Discrimination in Winnipeg High Schools." *Canadian Journal of Sociology* 6: 1–17.

———, and J. Peters. 1967. "Identity and Social Distance." *Canadian Review of Sociology and Anthropology* 14, 2: 158–173.

———, Charlene Thacker, and Raymond Currie. 1982. "Ethnic Identification: Variations in Regional and National Preferences." *Canadian Ethnic Studies* 14: 57–68.

Duleep, Harriet Orcutt, and Mark C. Regets. 1992. "Some Evidence on the Effects of Admissions Criteria on Immigrant Assimilation." In *Immigration, Language and Ethnicity: Canada and the United States*, edited by Barry R. Chiswick, 410–439. Washington, DC: AEI Press.

Elkins, David J. 1989. "Facing our Destiny: Rights and Canadian Distinctiveness." *Canadian Journal of Political Science* 22: 699–716.

Farley, Reynolds. 1983. *Catching Up: Recent Changes in the Social and Economic Status of Blacks.* Cambridge, Mass.: Harvard University Press.

———. 1984. *Blacks and Whites: Narrowing the Gap?* Cambridge, Mass.: Harvard University Press.

———, and Walter R. Allen. 1987. *The Color Line and the Quality of Life in America.* New York: The Russell Sage Foundation.

Featherman, David L., and Robert M. Hauser. 1978. *Opportunity and Change.* New York: Academic Press.

Fleras, A., and J.L. Elliott. 1992. *The Challenge of Diversity: Multiculturalism in Canada.* Scarborough, Ont.: Nelson Canada.

Fletcher, Joseph F. 1992. *Canadian Attitudes toward Competitiveness and Entrepreneurship.* Ottawa: Department of Industry, Science and Technology.

Fong, Eric. 1991. "A Comparative Perspective of Racial Residential Segregation: American and Canadian Experiences." Unpublished manuscript.

Gallup International Research Institute. 1977. *Human Needs and Satisfaction: A Global Survey.* Princeton, NJ, 1977.

Gans, Herbert J. 1979. "Symbolic Ethnicity: The Future of Ethnic Groups and Cultures." *Ethnic and Racial Studies* 2: 1–20.

Geschwender, James A. 1991. "State Policy, Immigration, Ethnicity, and Female Labour Force Participation: Report of a Comparison between Canada and the United States." State University of New York, Binghamton, NY, Department of Sociology and Institute for Research on Multiculturalism and International Labor. Research report submitted to Statistics Canada.

Gibbins, Roger, and Neil Nevitte. 1985. "Canadian Political Ideology: A Comparative Analysis." *Canadian Journal of Political Science* 18, 3: 577–598.

Glazer, Nathan, and Daniel P. Moynihan. [1963] 1970. *Beyond the Melting Pot: The Negroes, Puerto Ricans, Jews, Italians and Irish of New York City.* Second ed. Cambridge, Mass.: The MIT Press.

Glock, Charles Y., and Rodney Stark. 1966. *Christian Beliefs and Anti-Semitism.* New York: Harper and Row.

Goldlust, J., and A. Richmond. 1973. "A Multi-Variate Analysis of the Economic Adaptation of Immigrants in Toronto." Toronto: York University Institute of Behavioral Research. Research Report.

Goldstein, Jay, and Alexander Segall. 1985. "Ethnic Intermarriage and Ethnic Identity." *Canadian Ethnic Studies* 17: 60–71.

Greeley, Andrew M. 1976. *Ethnicity, Denomination and Inequality.* Beverly Hills, Calif.: Sage Publications.

Grubb, W. Norton, and Robert H. Wilson. 1989. "Sources of Increasing Inequality in Wages and Salaries, 1960–80." *Monthly Labor Review* 112, 4: 3–13.

Guppy, L. Neil. 1983–84. "Dissensus or Consensus: A Cross-National Comparison of Occupational Prestige Scales." *Canadian Journal of Sociology* 9: 69–83.

Gwartney, James E., and James L. Long. 1978. "The Earnings of Blacks and Other Minorities." *Industrial and Labor Relations Review* 31: 336–46.

Halli, Shiva S., Frank Trovato, and Leo Driedger, eds. 1990. *Ethnic Demography: Canadian Immigrant, Racial and Cultural Variations.* Ottawa: Carleton University Press.

Harris, Fred R., and Roger W. Wilkins, eds. 1988. *Quiet Riots: Race and Poverty in the United States: The Kerner Report Twenty Years Later.* New York: Pantheon Books.

Hastings, Elizabeth, and Philip K. Hastings, eds. 1982. *Index to International Public Opinion, 1980–81.* Westport Conn.: Greenwood Press.

Hechter, Michael. 1978. "Group Formation and the Cultural Division of Labor." *American Journal of Sociology* 84: 293–318.

Heckman, James J. 1979. "Sample Selection Bias as a Specification Error." *Econometrica* 47: 153–161.

————, and V. Joseph Hotz. 1986. "An Investigation of the Labor Market Earnings of Panamanian Males: Evaluating the Sources of Inequality." *Journal of Human Resources* 21: 507–42.

Henry, Frances. 1978. "The Dynamics of Racism in Toronto." Toronto: York University, Department of Anthropology. Mimeographed.

————. 1986. "Race Relations Research in Canada Today: A 'State of the Art' Review." Paper presented at the Canadian Human Rights Commission Colloquium on Racial Discrimination, Ottawa, September 25.

————. 1989. "Who Gets the Work in 1989?" Background Paper. Ottawa: Economic Council of Canada.

————, and Effie Ginsberg. 1985. *Who Gets the Work: A Test of Racial Discrimination in Employment.* Toronto: The Urban Alliance on Race Relations and the Social Planning Council of Metropolitan Toronto.

Hirschman, Charles. 1983. "America's Melting Pot Reconsidered." *Annual Review of Sociology* 9: 397–423.

Hofstede, Geert. 1984. *Culture's Consequences: International Differences in Work-Related Values.* Beverly Hills, Calif.: Sage Publications.

Hughes, David R., and Kallen, Evelyn. 1974. *The Anatomy of Racism: Canadian Dimensions.* Montreal: Harvest House.

Hughey, A.M. 1990. "The Incomes of Recent Female Immigrants in the United States." *Social Science Quarterly* 71: 383–390.

Inglehart, Ronald. 1990. *Culture Shift in Advanced Industrial Society.* Princeton, NJ: Princeton University Press.

Iredale, R.R. 1988. *Wasted Skills: Barriers to Migrant Entry to Occupations in Australia.* Sydney: Ethnic Affairs Commission of New South Wales.

Isajiw, Wsevolod W. 1990. "Ethnic-Identity Retention." In Raymond Breton et al. *Ethnic Identity and Inequality: Varieties of Experience in a Canadian City*, 34–91. Toronto: University of Toronto Press.

Jain, Harish. 1989. "Racial Minorities and Affirmative Action/Employment Equity Legislation in Canada." *Industrial Relations* 44, 3: 593–613.

————, and P.J. Sloane. 1981. *Equal Employment Issues: Race and Sex Discrimination in the United States, Canada, and Britain.* New York: Praeger.

Jasso, Guillermina, and Mark R. Rosensweig. 1988. "How Well Do US Immigrants Do? Vintage Effects, Emigration Selectivity, and Occupational Mobility." *Research in Population Economics* 6: 229–253.

Jaynes, Gerald David, and Robin M. Williams, Jr. 1989. *A Common Destiny: Blacks and American Society.* Washington, DC: National Academy Press.

Jiobu, Robert M. 1990. *Ethnicity and Inequality*. Albany: State University of New York Press.

Johnson, James H., and Melvin L. Oliver. 1989. "Interethnic Minority Conflict in Urban America: The Effects of Economic and Social Dislocations." *Urban Geography* 10, 5: 449–463.

Kalbach, Warren E. 1970. *The Impact of Immigration on Canada's Population*. Ottawa: Dominion Bureau of Statistics, Queen's Printer.

Kluegel, James R. 1985. "'If There Isn't a Problem, You Don't Need a Solution': The Bases of Contemporary Affirmative Action Attitudes." *American Behavioral Scientist* 28: 761–84.

————. 1990. "Trends in Whites' Explanations of the Black-White Gap in Socioeconomic Status, 1977–1989." *American Sociological Review* 55, 4: 512–525.

————, and Eliot R. Smith. 1986. *Beliefs about Inequality: Americans' Views of What Is and What Ought to Be*. New York: Aldine de Gruyter.

Kobayashi, Audrey. 1992. "The Japanese-Canadian Redress Settlement and its Implications for 'Race Relations.'" *Canadian Ethnic Studies* 26, 1: 1–19.

Kralt, John. 1977. *Ethnic Origins of Canadians*. 1971 Census of Canada Profile Studies, Volume V, Part 1. Ottawa: Queen's Printer.

————. 1980. "Ethnic Origin in the Canadian Census, 1871–1981." In *Changing Realities: Social Trends Among Ukrainian Canadians*, edited by W. Roman Petryshyn, 18–49. Edmonton: The Canadian Institute of Ukrainian Studies.

————. 1990. "Ethnic Origins in the Canadian Census." In *Ethnic Demography: Canadian Immigrant, Racial and Cultural Variations*, edited by Shiva S. Halli, Frank Trovato, and Leo Driedger, 13–29. Ottawa: Carleton University Press.

————, and Ravi Pendakur. 1991. *Ethnicity, Immigration and Language Transfer*. Ottawa: Department of Multiculturalism and Citizenship.

Krotki, Karol J., and Dave Odynak. 1990. "The Emergence of Multiethnicities in the Eighties." In *Ethnic Demography: Canadian Immigrant, Racial and Cultural Variations*, edited by Shiva S. Halli, Frank Trovato, and Leo Driedger, 415–437. Ottawa: Carleton University Press.

Kumar, Pradeep. 1993. *From Uniformity to Divergence: Industrial Relations in Canada and the United States*. Kingston, Ont.: Industrial Relations Centre, Queen's University.

Lachapelle, Réjean. 1980. "Evolution of Ethnic and Linguistic Composition." In *Cultural Boundaries and the Cohesion of Canada*, edited by

Raymond Breton, Jeffrey G. Reitz, and Victor F. Valentine, 15–40. Montreal: Institute for Research on Public Policy.

Lambert, Ronald, and James Curtis. 1984. "Québécois and English Canadian Opposition to Racial and Religious Intermarriage, 1968–1983." *Canadian Ethnic Studies* 16, 2: 30–46.

Lambert, Wallace E., Josiane F. Hamers, and Nancy Frasure-Smith. 1979. *Child Rearing Values: A Cross-National Study.* New York: Praeger.

League for Human Rights of B'Nai Brith Canada. 1991. *1991 Audit of Anti-Semitic Incidents.* Downsview, Ont.: The League.

Li, Peter S. 1988. *Ethnic Inequality in a Class Society.* Toronto: Wall and Thompson.

Lieberson, Stanley. 1985. "Unhyphenated Whites in the United States." *Ethnic and Racial Studies* 8: 159–180.

———, and Mary Waters. 1988. *From Many Strands: Ethnic and Racial Groups in Contemporary America.* New York: Russell Sage Foundation.

Lipset, Seymour M. 1963. *The First New Nation.* New York: Basic Books.

———. 1989. *Continental Divide: The Values and Institutions of the United States and Canada.* Toronto; Washington, DC: Canadian-American Committee.

McClosky, Herbert, and John Zaller. 1984. *The American Ethos: Public Attitudes toward Capitalism and Democracy.* Cambridge, Mass.: Harvard University Press.

Maclean's. 1989. "Portrait of Two Nations: The Dreams and Ideals of Canadians and Americans." July 3, 23–82.

———. 1990. "Portrait of Two Nations: Should the Two Countries Become One?" June 25, 37–52.

McNaught, Kenneth. 1966. "American Progressives and the Great Society." *Journal of American History* 53 (December), 504–520.

McRoberts, H.A., and K. Selbee. 1981. "Trends in Occupational Mobility: Canada and the US" *American Sociological Review* 46: 406–421.

Martire, Gregory, and Ruth Clark. 1982. *Anti-Semitism in the United States: A Study of Prejudice in the 1980s.* New York: Praeger.

Megyery, Kathy, ed. 1991. *Ethno-Cultural Groups and Visible Minorities in Canadian Politics: The Question of Access.* Report of the Royal Commission on Electoral Reform and Party Financing and Canada Communications Group. Ottawa: Supply and Services Canada and Dundurn Press.

Meltz, Noah M. 1989. "Interstate vs. Interprovincial Differences in Union Density." *Industrial Relations* 28, 2: 142–158.

Michalos, Alex C. 1982. *North American Social Report: A Comparative Study of the Quality of Life in Canada and the USA from 1964 to 1974*, Vol. 5., *Economics, Religion and Morality*. Dordrecht, Netherlands: D. Reidel.

Miki, Roy, and Cassandra Kobayashi. 1991. *Justice in Our Time: The Japanese-Canadian Redress Settlement*. Vancouver: Talonbooks; Winnipeg: National Association of Japanese-Canadians.

Model, Suzanne. 1991. "Caribbean Immigrants: A Black Success Story?" *International Migration Review* 25, 2: 248–276.

Myrdal, Gunnar. 1944. *An American Dilemma: The Negro Problem and Modern Democracy*. New York: Harper and Row.

Nakamura, Alice, and Masao Nakamura. 1992. "Wage Rates of Immigrant and Native Men in Canada and the United States." In *Immigration, Language and Ethnicity: Canada and the United States*, edited by Barry R. Chiswick, 145–166. Washington, DC: AEI Press.

Niemi, Richard G., John Mueller, and Tom W. Smith. 1989. *Trends in Public Opinion: A Compendium of Survey Data*. New York: Greenwood Press.

O'Bryan, K.G., J.G. Reitz, and O.M. Kuplowska. 1976. *Non-Official Languages: A Study in Canadian Multiculturalism*. Ottawa: Supply and Services Canada.

O'Hare, William P. 1992. "America's Minorities — The Demographics of Diversity." *Population Bulletin* 47, 4: 2–47.

Oliver, Melvin L., and Mark A. Glick. 1982. "An Analysis of the New Orthodoxy on Black Mobility." *Social Problems* 29, 5: 511–523.

———, and James H. Johnson, Jr. 1984. "Inter-Ethnic Conflict in an Urban Ghetto: The Case of Blacks and Latinos in Los Angeles." *Research in Social Movements, Conflict and Change* 6: 57–94.

Olzak Susan. 1983. "Contemporary Ethnic Mobilization." *Annual Review of Sociology* 9: 355–374.

———, and Joanne Nagel, eds. 1986. *Competitive Ethnic Relations*. Orlando: Academic Press.

Owen, Carolyn, Howard C. Eisner, and Thomas R. McFaul. 1981. "A Half-Century of Social Distance Research: National Replication of the Bogardus' Studies." *Sociology and Social Research* 66, 1: 80–98.

Palmer, Howard. 1976. "Mosaic versus Melting Pot? Immigration and Ethnicity in Canada and the United States." *International Journal* 31, Summer: 488–528.

————. 1982. *Patterns of Prejudice*. Toronto: McClelland and Stewart.

Peter, Karl. 1981. "The Myth of Multiculturalism and Other Political Fables." In *Ethnicity, Power, and Politics in Canada*, edited by Jorgen Dahlie and Tessa Fernando, 56–67. Toronto: Methuen.

Pineo, P. 1977. "The Social Standing of Ethnic and Racial Groupings." *Canadian Review of Sociology and Anthropology* 14: 147–57.

————, and John Porter. 1973. "Occupational Prestige in Canada." In *Social Stratification in Canada*, edited by James E. Curtis and William G. Scott, 59–68. Scarborough, Ont.: Prentice-Hall Canada.

Piore, Michael J. 1979. *Birds of Passage: Migrant Labor and Industrial Societies*. Cambridge.: Cambridge University Press.

Ponting, Rick. 1986. Unpublished survey data.

Porter, John. 1965. *The Vertical Mosaic: An Analysis of Class and Power in Canada*. Toronto: University of Toronto Press.

————. 1975. "Ethnic Pluralism in Canadian Perspective." In *Ethnicity: Theory and Experience*, edited by Nathan Glazer and Patrick Moynihan, 267–304. Cambridge, Mass.: Harvard University Press.

————. 1979. "Melting Pot or Mosaic: Revolution or Reversion?" In *The Measure of Canadian Society: Education, Equality, Opportunity*, edited by John Porter, 139–162. Toronto: Gage.

Porter, Michael. 1991. *Canada at the Crossroads: The Reality of a New Competitive Environment*. Ottawa Business Council on National Issues and Supply and Services Canada.

Portes, Alejandro, and John Walton. 1981. *Labor, Class, and the International System*. New York: Academic Press.

Pryor, Edward T., et al. 1992. "Measuring Ethnicity: Is 'Canadian' an Evolving Indigenous Category?" *Ethnic and Racial Studies* 15: 214–235.

Reimers, Cordelia. 1983. "Labor Market Discrimination Against Hispanic and Black Men." *Review of Economics and Statistics* 65: 570–559.

————. 1985. "A Comparative Analysis of the Wages of Hispanics, Blacks, and Non-Hispanic Whites." In *Hispanics in the U.S. Economy*, edited by George Borjas and Marta Tienda, 27–75. Orlando, Fla.: Academic Press.

Reimers, David M., and Harold Troper. 1992. "Canadian and American Immigration Policy since 1945." In *Immigration, Language and Ethnicity: Canada and the United States*, edited by Barry R. Chiswick, 15–54. Washington, DC: AEI Press.

Reitz, Jeffrey G. 1980a. "Immigrants, their Descendants, and the Cohesion of Canada." In *Cultural Boundaries and the Cohesion of Canada*, edited by Raymond Breton, Jeffrey G. Reitz, and Victor Valentine, 329–417. Montreal: Institute for Research on Public Policy.

———. 1980b. *The Survival of Ethnic Groups*. Toronto: McGraw-Hill Ryerson.

———.1988a. "The Institutional Structure of Immigration as a Determinant of Inter-Racial Competition: A Comparison of Britain and Canada." *International Migration Review* 22, 1: 117–146.

———. 1988b. "Less Racial Discrimination in Canada, or Simply Less Racial Conflict? Implications of Comparisons with Britain." *Canadian Public Policy* 14, 4: 424–441.

———. 1990. "Ethnic Concentrations in Labor Markets and Their Implications for Ethnic Inequality." In Raymond Breton, Wsevolod Isajiw, Warren E. Kalbach, and Jeffrey G. Reitz, *Ethnic Identity and Inequality: Varieties of Experience in a Canadian City*, 135–195. Toronto: University of Toronto Press.

———. 1993. "Statistics on Racial Discrimination in Canada." *Policy Options* 14, 2: 32–36.

———. 1994. "A Comment on de Silva and Palmer." *Policy Options* 15, 2: 7–9.

Richard, Madeline A. 1991. *Ethnic Groups and Marital Choices*. Vancouver: University of British Columbia Press.

———. Forthcoming. "Intermarriage." In Warren Kalbach and Madeline A. Richard, *The Ethnic Connection in Canada*.

Richmond, Anthony H., and Warren Kalbach. 1980. *Factors in the Adjustment of Immigrants and Their Descendants*. Ottawa: Statistics Canada.

Rokeach, Milton. 1974. "Some Reflections about the Place of Values in Canadian Social Science." In *Perspectives on the Social Sciences in Canada*, edited by T.N. Guinsberg and G.L. Reuber, 152–190. Toronto: University of Toronto Press.

Rose, Harold M. 1989. "Blacks and Cubans in Metropolitan Miami's Changing Economy." *Urban Geography* 10, 5: 464–486.

Schlesinger, Arthur M., Jr. 1992. *The Disuniting of America: Reflections on a Multicultural Society*. New York: W.W. Norton.

Schoenfeld, Stuart. 1991. "Hate Groups, Hate Propaganda and Racial Conflict." Unpublished manuscript.

Schuman, Howard, Charlotte Steeh, and Lawrence Bobo. 1985. *Racial Attitudes in America: Trends and Interpretations.* Cambridge, Mass.: Harvard University Press.

Seltzer, Rick, and Grace M. Lopes. 1986. "The Ku Klux Klan: Reasons for Support or Opposition Among White Respondents." *Journal of Black Studies* 17, 1: 91–109.

Shefman, Alan. 1987. "Manifestations of Anti-Semitism in Canada: The 1987 Survey." In *The Review of Anti-Semitism in Canada*, edited by Frank Chalk, 3–7. Downsview, Ont.: League for Human Rights of B'nai Brith Canada.

Sher, Julian. 1983. *White Hoods: Canada's Ku Klux Klan.* Vancouver: New Star Books.

Simon, Julian L. 1989. *The Economic Consequences of Immigration.* Oxford; New York: Basil Blackwell.

Sinha, Murli M., and Brian Berry. 1991. "Ethnicity, Stigmatized Groups and Social Distance: An Expanded Update of the Bogardus Scale." Paper presented at the annual meetings of the American Sociological Association, Cincinnati, August 23–27.

Smith, Allan. 1970. "Metaphor and Nationality in North America." *The Canadian Historical Review* 51, 3: 247–275.

Smith, James P. 1984. "Race and Human Capital." *American Economic Review* 74, 4: 685–698.

———, and Finis R. Welch. 1989. "Black Economic Progress After Myrdal." *Journal of Economic Literature* 27: 519–564.

Smith, Tom W. 1980. "Ethnic Measurement and Identification." *Ethnicity* 7: 78–95.

———. 1990. "Ethnic Images." GSS Topical Report no. 19, National Opinion Research Center, University of Chicago.

Sniderman, Paul M. 1993. "Psychological and Cultural Foundations of Prejudice: The Case of Anti-Semitism in Quebec." *Canadian Review of Sociology and Anthropology* 30, 2: 242–270.

———, and Michael G. Hagen. 1985. *Race and Inequality: A Study in American Values.* Chatham, NJ: Chatham House.

———, et al. 1991. "Political Culture and the Problem of Double Standards: Mass and Elite Attitudes Toward Language Rights in the Canadian Charter of Rights and Freedoms." *Canadian Journal of Political Science* 22, 2: 259–284.

————, et al. 1992. "Working Paper on Anti-Semitism in Quebec." Toronto: York University Institute for Survey Research.

Stark, Rodney, and Charles Y. Glock. 1968. *American Piety: The Nature of Religious Commitment*. Berkeley: University of California Press.

Statistics Canada. 1984. *1981 Census of Canada. Population: Ethnic Origin*. Ottawa: Supply and Services Canada.

————. 1992. *Changing Faces: Visible Minorities in Toronto*. Ottawa: Statistics Canada.

————. 1993. *1991 Census of Canada. Ethnic Origin: The Nation*. Ottawa: Industry, Science and Technology Canada.

Stevens, Gillian. 1985. "Nativity, Intermarriage, and Mother Tongue Shift." *American Sociological Review* 50: 74–83.

————. 1992. "The Social and Demographic Context of Language Use in the United States." *American Sociological Review* 57: 171–185.

————, and Gray Swicegood. 1987. "The Linguistic Context of Ethnic Endogamy." *American Sociological Review* 52: 73–82.

Stier, Haya. 1991. "Immigrant Women Go to Work: Analysis of Immigrant Wives' Labor Supply for Six Asian Groups." *Social Science Quarterly* 72: 67–82.

Stolzenberg, Ross M. 1975. "Education, Occupation, and Wage Differences between White and Black Men." *American Journal of Sociology* 81, 2: 299–323.

Swan, Neil, et al. 1991. *Economic and Social Impacts of Immigration: A Research Report Prepared for the Economic Council of Canada*. Ottawa: Supply and Services Canada.

Terkel, Studs. 1992. *Race: How Blacks and Whites Think and Feel about the American Obsession*. New York: Doubleday Anchor.

Tienda, Marta, and Ding-Tzann Lii. 1987. "Minority Concentration and Earnings Inequality: Blacks, Hispanics, and Asians Compared." *American Journal of Sociology* 93, 1: 141–165.

Tocqueville, Alexis de. [1835 and 1840] 1945. *Democracy in America*, 2 vols. New York: Vintage Books.

Treiman, Donald J., et al. 1986–87. *"Occupational Status Attainment among Ethnic Groups in Los Angeles*. Working Papers in the Social Sciences, vol. 2, no. 1. Los Angeles: Institute for Social Research, University of California.

————, and Hye-kyung Lee. 1988. "Income Differences among 28 Ethnic Groups in Los Angeles." Paper presented at the annual meeting of the Population Association of America, New Orleans, April.

Turner, Margey Austin, Michael Fix, and Raymond J. Struyk. 1991. *Opportunities Denied, Opportunities Diminished: Discrimination in Hiring*. Washington: Urban Institute Project.

United States. 1989. *Population Estimates by Race and Hispanic Origin for States, Metropolitan Areas, and Selected Counties: 1980–1985*. Current Population Reports, series P-25, no. 1040-RD-1. Washington, DC: US Government Printing Office.

————. Bureau of the Census. 1983. *Ancestry of the Population by States, 1980*. Supplementary report no. PC80-S1-10. Washington, DC: US Government Printing Office.

————. Bureau of the Census. 1992. *1990 Census of Population and Housing. Summary Tape File 3A [Computer File]*. Washington, DC: Department of Commerce, Bureau of the Census, Data User Services Division.

Vaillancourt, François. 1989. "Demolinguistic Trends and Canadian Institutions." In *Demolinguistic Trends and the Evolution of Canadian Institutions*, 73–92. Association for Canadian Studies, Department of the Secretary of State, and the Office of the Commissioner for Official Languages, Montreal.

Veltman, Calvin. 1983. *Language Shift in the United States*. New York: Mouton.

Verma, R.B.P., and K.G. Basavarajappa. 1989. "Employment Income of Immigrants in Metropolitan Areas of Canada, 1980". *International Migration* 27, 3: 441–465.

Waldinger, Roger. 1989. "Race and Ethnicity." In *Setting Municipal Priorities, 1990*, edited by Charles Brecher and Raymond D. Horton, 50–78. New York: New York University Press.

Waters, Mary. 1991a. "The Dilemma of the Second Generation: Caribbean Immigrants in the United States." Presentation at the Robert F. Harney Professorship and Program in Ethnic, Immigration and Pluralism Studies, University of Toronto, November 1991.

————. 1991b. "The Intersection Between Race and Ethnicity: Generational Changes among Caribbean Immigrants to the United States." Paper presented at the annual meeting of the American Sociological Association, Cincinnati, August 23.

Weinfeld, Morton. 1981. "Myth and Reality in the Canadian Mosaic: 'Affective Ethnicity'." *Canadian Ethnic Studies* 13: 80–100.

Wilson, William J. 1978. *The Declining Significance of Race.* Chicago: University of Chicago Press.

———. 1987. *The Truly Disadvantaged: The Inner City, the Underclass, and Public Policy.* Chicago: University of Chicago Press.

Woodsworth, J.S. [1909] 1972. *Strangers Within Our Gates.* Reprint. Toronto: University of Toronto Press.

Yancey, William B., Eugene P. Ericksen, and Richard N. Juliani. 1976. "Emergent Ethnicity: A Review and Reformulation." *American Sociological Review* 41: 391–403.

Members of the
C.D. Howe Institute[*]

[*] The views expressed in this publication are those of the authors and do not necessarily reflect the opinions of the Institute's members.

Consumers Gas
Coopers & Lybrand
E. Kendall Cork
William J. Cosgrove
Co-Steel Inc.
Pierre Côté
Cott Corporation
J.G. Crean
Crestbrook Forest Industries Ltd.
John Crispo
Devon Gaffney Cross
Crown Life Insurance Company Limited
Thomas P. d'Aquino
Leo de Bever
W. Ross DeGeer
Deloitte & Touche
Desjardins Ducharme Stein Monast
Robert Després
Deutsche Bank (Canada)
John H. Dickey
Iain St. C. Dobson
The Dominion of Canada General
    Insurance Company
Du Pont Canada Inc.
Marcel Dutil
Gordon H. Eberts
The Empire Life Insurance Company
H.E. English
ENSIS Corporation
Ernst & Young
Export Development Corporation
Ronald J. Farano, Q.C.
Field & Field Perraton Masuch
First Marathon Securities Limited
Aaron M. Fish
John P. Fisher
Fishery Products International Limited
C.J. Michael Flavell, Q.C.
Fleck Manufacturing Inc.
Ford Motor Company of Canada, Limited
Formula Growth Limited
L. Yves Fortier, C.C., Q.C.
Four Seasons Hotels Limited
GSW Inc.
Hilary Geller
General Electric Canada Inc.
General Motors of Canada Limited

Gluskin Sheff + Associates Inc.
Goodman & Goodman
Peter Goring
The Great-West Life Assurance Company
Greyhound Lines of Canada
Morton Gross
Le Groupe Secor Inc.
Groupe Sobeco Inc.
H. Anthony Hampson
C.M. Harding Foundation
Lawrence L. Herman
Hewlett-Packard (Canada) Ltd.
Hill & Knowlton Canada
Hollinger Inc.
Home Oil Company Limited
Gordon J. Homer
Honeywell Limited
Hongkong Bank of Canada
The Horsham Corporation
Dezsö Horváth
Human Resources Association of
    Nova Scotia
H. Douglas Hunter
Hydro-Québec
IBM Canada Ltd.
Imasco Limited
Imperial Oil Limited
Inco Limited
Inland Cement Limited
The Insurance Bureau of Canada
Interprovincial Pipe Line Inc.
Investors Group Inc.
IPSCO Inc.
Tsutomu Iwasaki
The Jarislowsky Foundation
Robert Johnstone
KPMG Peat Marwick Thorne
Joseph Kruger II
Lac Minerals Ltd.
R.William Lawson
Jacques A. Lefebvre
Gérard Limoges
London Life Insurance Company
J.W. (Wes) MacAleer
McCallum Hill Companies
McCarthy Tétrault
MacDonald, Dettwiler & Associates Ltd.

McKinsey & Company
Maclab Enterprises
James Maclaren Industries Inc.
Maclean Hunter Limited
Jack M. MacLeod
McMillan Binch
MacMillan Bloedel Limited
William Mackness
Mannville Oil & Gas Ltd.
The Manufacturers Life Insurance
Company
Maple Leaf Foods Inc.
Maritime Telegraph & Telephone
Company, Limited
Marsh & McLennan Limited
Master Equity Investments Inc.
James Mauldin
The Mercantile and General
Reinsurance Group
William M. Mercer Limited
Merck Frosst Canada Inc.
Ronald H. Meredith-Jones
Methanex Corporation
Micmac Maliseet Development
Corporation Inc.
Miles Canada Inc.
Robert Mitchell Inc.
The Molson Companies Limited
Monsanto Canada Inc.
Montreal Trust
Moore Corporation Limited
The Mutual Life Assurance Company of
Canada
National Trust
National Westminster Bank of Canada
Nesbitt Thomson Deacon
Noma Industries Limited
Noranda Forest Inc.
Noranda Inc.
North American Life Assurance Company
Northwood Pulp and Timber Limited
NOVA Corporation of Alberta
Ontario Hydro
The Oshawa Group Limited
James S. Palmer
PanCanadian Petroleum Limited
Pembina Corporation
Petro-Canada

Philips, Hager & North Ltd.
Les Placements T.A.L. Ltée.
Placer Dome Inc.
David A. Potts
Power Corporation of Canada
PowerWest Financial Ltd.
Pratt & Whitney Canada Inc.
Price Waterhouse
J. Robert S. Prichard
Procor Limited
ProGas Limited
QUNO Corporation
RBC Dominion Securities Inc.
Redpath Industries Limited
Henri Remmer
Retail Council of Canada
Richardson Greenshields
of Canada Limited
R.T. Riley
Robin Hood Multifoods Inc.
Rogers Communications Inc.
Rothschild Canada Limited
Royal Bank of Canada
ROYCO Hotels & Resorts
St. Lawrence Cement Inc.
Samuel, Son & Co., Limited
Sandwell Inc.
Sanpalo Investments Corporation
Guylaine Saucier
André Saumier
Sceptre Investment Counsel
Sceptre Resources Limited
Dick Schmeelk
ScotiaMcLeod Inc.
Sierra Systems Consultants Inc.
Sharwood and Company
Shell Canada Limited
Sherritt Inc.
Sidbec-Dosco Inc.
Southam Inc.
Spar Aerospace Limited
Speedy Muffler King Inc.
Speirs Consultants Inc.
Philip Spencer, Q.C.
The Standard Life Assurance Company
Strategico Inc.
Sun Life Assurance Company of Canada